CLASSROOM MANAGEMENT

Philip Waterhouse

Network Educational Press

Network Educational Press
Network House
PO Box 635
Stafford
ST18 0LJ

First published 1990
© Network Educational Press

ISBN 85539 004 3

Acknowledgements

Philip Waterhouse would like to acknowledge his involvement with the
Avon Resources for Learning Project, where many of the ideas
expressed in this book were first developed, and with CET's Supported
Self Study project where many of the ideas were refined. This book
takes much further some of the issues raised in one of his earlier books,
"Managing the Learning process", published by McGraw Hill in 1983
and now out of print.

Contents

INTRODUCTION

A   ## What is Classroom Management?

The average person in the street has a clear picture of teaching. It consists of a teacher standing in front of a large number of students in a classroom *telling* them. It is simply a matter of teachers *talking* and students *listening*. If only teachers would *tell* them more and *make them listen*, educational standards would improve. Teachers know that the reality is different. The 'person in the street' is ignoring some facts of life.

- [ ] **The students are all different from each other.**
  The pace at which they can work, the depth to which they can understand, the background of knowledge and experience that they bring, their attitude and willingness to learn - all these vary enormously from one student to another.

- [ ] **The aims and objectives of education are numerous and complex.**
  They go well beyond the acquisition of simple knowledge and are concerned with the total development of the whole person.

- [ ] **The demands and pressures that come from society are often confused and self-contradictory.**
  It is easy to make the headlines with a demand for a particular emphasis in learning or in discipline or in school organisation. It is much more difficult to accomplish all the needs of society in a balanced and constructive way inside a single classroom.

- [ ] **The classroom environment is multidimensional**
  There are so many different events and so many different tasks.

- [ ] **Things happen simultaneously!**
  The teacher in the classroom is rarely dealing with one situation or event in isolation. Considerable skill is required to handle this. Successful teachers are extremely alert and often display flair which defies analysis.

- [ ] **The pace is fast.**
  There is very little time for the teacher to reflect, or to plan, or to analyse in depth.

□   **Many of the events of classroom life are unpredictable.**
It is not only that students create problems by their unpredictable
behaviour, but also that their intellectual responses, even when
they are cooperative, may be different to those expected.

□   **Everything that happens in the classroom is public.**
This tends to inhibit sensitive adjustment and common sense
compromises. Students and teacher alike often find it difficult to
avoid the 'adversarial' style.

So classroom life is not simple. The teacher is trying to achieve a
number of objectives in the classroom simultaneously:

- Provide the students with a wide range of learning experiences -
  as members of the whole class, as members of small groups, and
  as individuals.

- Make adequate provision for individual differences by providing
  a wide choice of learning resources, differentiated tasks, and
  varying levels of assessment.

- Keep adequate records of the progress of individual students.

- Make sure that the learning programme is well-balanced and
  satisfies the requirements of the National Curriculum.

- Provide opportunity for students to take responsibility for the
  management of their own learning through decision making as
  individuals and as members of groups.

- Provide a balanced style of management and control. So much
  debate about education is polarised: *progressive* versus
  traditional, discipline versus *freedom* , *choice* versus *prescription*.
  Teachers tend not to identify with any of these positions,
  preferring instead the more difficult task of striking a decent
  balance.

This is formidable enough. But there are added complications.

These arise, paradoxically, from valuable work during the last two
decades which has been designed to improve the quality of teaching and
learning. Much of the thinking and experimentation has led to the
development of *systems* of teaching and learning. Most of these have
been based on the student-centred philosophy, with its concern for
individual differences and for the ultimate goal of student autonomy.
There is much to commend. But each system has presented its own
distinctive argument. Many of the following will be familiar.

THE SYSTEM	ITS BASIC ARGUMENT
Resource-based learning.	Learning materials are now widely available and in a variety of interesting media. Students should be trained to access information and ideas themselves, rather than being dependent on the teacher as the sole source of information and ideas. In this way the students are progressing towards ultimate autonomy.
Open Learning	Access to education should be freely available and students should be encouraged to seek new learning when, where, and in what manner is best for them. This implies that institutions should become more flexible ín their arrangements. Some students should be encouraged to study independently away from the conventional class times and places.
Supported Self-Study	Young students progressing towards greater responsibility need to work for some of the time independently. But they cannot be expected to acquire the techniques and strategies of the independent learner without skilled support and without training.
Active Learning	Young students learn best when they are active, and not merely trying to absorb ideas and information passively. This means that classroom work should be centred round the activity of the students. So the teacher's agenda must be designed with student activity in mind.
Experiential Learning	Young students need to enlarge their first-hand experiences of real life and use these as the basis for their learning. So much learning will take place outside the classroom.

3

Flexible Learning

The varying needs of students demand that the teacher responds with flexibility using a variety of different resources and methods. And institutions, at all levels, need to create environments which encourage and support flexibility both by the teachers and by the students themselves.

Records of Achievement

All student achievements and experiences should be recorded by a school, not just the academic. The student should be involved in assembling the information, making the necessary judgements, and keeping the records. The record of achievement implies a continuous process of consultation and negotiation. It is student-centred and promotes student responsibility.

Many of these ideas have been taken up and incorporated into government plans and initiatives.

The Technical and Vocational Education Initiative (TVEI)
The Certificate of Pre-vocational Education (CPVE)

The General Certificate of Secondary Education (GCSE)

The National Curriculum

The initiatives for the 16-19 age group - core skills and the integration of academic and vocational education

---

It is a pity that, in the minds of some teachers, this proliferation of systems and initiatives has led to confusion. But it would certainly be nonsense for teachers to regard them as competing with each other.

Each system has its own emphasis and appeal, and each has made a valuable contribution to the thinking and to developments within the major government initiatives. But they are all using the same focus. They are student-centred and therefore concerned with individual differences and needs, and with progressive training in greater responsibility. They are members of the same family. *So teachers would be well advised not to identify with any one system but to use the insights gained from them all.*

This would result in teaching and learning which includes these characteristics:

From resource-based learning The use of a wide variety of learning resources (multimedia) both within the classroom and beyond it. There would be a strong emphasis on information and study skills acquired through on-the-job training.

From open learning The use of open learning facilities both within the institution and without. Students would be encouraged to make their own responsible decisions (according to their age and experience) about when, where and how they worked.

From supported self-study The support of skilful tutoring designed to promote the responsible participation of the students and to enhance the quality of their independent work.

From active learning The use of active learning techniques, both within the normal class teaching and within the individual and small group work which supports it.

From experiential learning The use of first-hand experience as an essential way of getting the data and stimuli on which the learning experiences will be built.

From flexible learning The setting up of flexible arrangements for learning, both within the classroom and within the whole institution.

From records of achievement The involvement of students in the formation of their own comprehensive records as an integral part of the learning process.

Of course, the demands that all this makes on the teacher are considerable. It requires managerial skills of a high order. The teacher's work in the classroom is extraordinarily complex. *It is very different from the layman's image of teaching.*

So the term *classroom management* is intended to emphasise the variety and complexity of classroom life, and to focus on the wide range of managerial skills that the modern teacher needs to have. It is not a system of teaching, it is instead a systematic way of coordinating the variety and complexity which is inevitable in the modern classroom.

So the teacher is a *manager,* co-ordinating a varied and complex environment, looking constantly at the great managerial issues -

- Setting objectives,
- Planning structures and procedures,
- Attending to communications and motivation,
- Evaluating performance.

The teacher really is a *manager*. But lest any doubt remains it is worth recording that the idea has actually been expressed the other way round!

Peter Drucker, the eminent management consultant and writer, was attempting to answer the question: *What does it mean to be a manager?* After considerable intellectual effort he summed it all up in this single sentence!

> Being a manager, though, is more like being a parent, or a teacher.

(Peter Drucker. The Practice of Management. Pan.)

B Implementing Classroom Management

There are not many really new ideas in education. Most of the basic principles of student-centred learning have been advocated for a long time. The trouble is that a lot of the advice and exhortation stops short at the classroom door. The teacher is left with a long list of objectives and imperatives and a big task of sorting and coordinating.

Nevertheless many teachers are involved to a greater or lesser degree in student-centred approaches. Good practice is widespread. Converting teachers to student-centred thinking is not the problem it is often made out to be. At too many educational conferences speakers are inclined to dwell on the problem of 'teacher attitudes'. While this may still be partially true it is a smoke-screen covering the real problem.

The real problem for teachers is how to build up a wide repertoire of skills and techniques, how to organise these into useful structures and styles, and how to maximise the potential of the limited time and resources at their disposal. This is the problem of classroom management. It highlights the complexity of the teacher's work. Its need is most apparent in the large classes of the lower school where large numbers and the immaturity of the students combine to present the biggest challenge to managerial skills.

To bring about improvements in classroom management an individual teacher can accomplish much working alone, but it is much better if a collaborative approach can be used. A team of teachers (a department or faculty, a year group) is likely to be the most effective unit, but such teams need to be supported by whole school policies and practice.

The Cycle of Improvement

The improvement of teaching and learning is not a one-off action. It is an on-going cyclical activity. Within such a cycle there is a thinking and planning stage which is followed by an action stage. This is followed by another thinking and planning stage, and so on. The diagram demonstrates the components of the basic cycle.

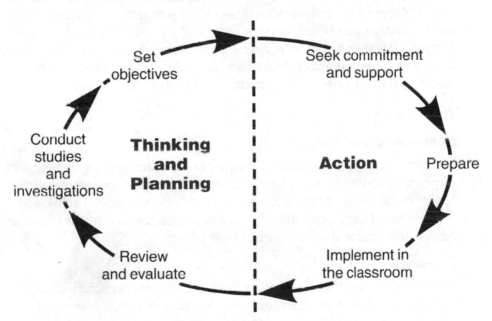

Set objectives

Seek commitment and support

Conduct studies and investigations

Thinking and Planning

Action　　Prepare

Review and evaluate

Implement in the classroom

The Systematic Improvement of Classroom Management

The Thinking and Planning Stage

Review and Evaluation

This is the start of thinking and planning. The teachers look back over the last term (or year) and ask themselves questions. What actually happened? What improvements did we succeed in making to the quality of teaching and learning? Where could we have done better?

Studies and Investigations

With the evaluation complete the dissatisfactions, uncertainties, problems, and opportunities will have surfaced. Some of these may require further study and investigation. Some teachers might be asked to plan and negotiate cross-curricular work; some might study new techniques in methods or in technology. There will be visits, attendance at courses, and reading.

Objectives

The planning of next year's improvements can now go ahead. The way to use objectives is to be selective and to be practical. The question to ask is simply this: *What improvements will we see in teaching and learning between the present time and the next review?* In other words, keep it small and manageable; this is not the occasion for massive documentation or for major statements of philosophy!

The Action Stage

Commitment and Support

The first task of the Action Stage is to get the commitment and support of people outside the team itself - students, parents, other teachers, the senior management team, LEA advisers. By *going public* in this way the resolve of the team members becomes stronger, and much valuable advice and practical help may be obtained.

Preparation

Detailed decision-making now follows. The actual preparation may include new resources, learning activities, tests, record systems, or changes to the layout of classrooms.

The Teaching

When a team of teachers has gone through this kind of collaborative preparation the teaching itself is conducted with greater resolve and mutual aid.

The Benefits of the Cycle

It is a disciplined way of bringing about improvements.

Because it has been planned and is deliberate it serves as a constant reminder and a checklist. It focuses attention on what is important.

It is a cooperative way of working.

Members of a team find it intellectually stimulating and helpful to interpersonal relations.

It introduces objectivity into classroom improvements.

Teaching is such an intensely personal thing that critical analysis is a delicate and dangerous business. It is only when teachers have personally chosen objectives and gained the support of their colleagues that they will feel relaxed in the evaluation of their performance.

It is cumulative

The cycle never ends. Improvements made in one cycle become the base line for improvements in the next.

1

A Framework of
Classroom Management

The Components of classroom management

The Design of classroom activities

A FRAMEWORK OF CLASSROOM MANAGEMENT

This chapter is designed to give an overview of classroom management. It provides a firm framework for the detail which will follow in later chapters.

A

The Components of Classroom Management

One important characteristic of good teaching is its **variety.** Young people do not thrive on a monotonous diet, however well it is presented. So teachers try to vary the classroom experiences as much as possible. The range of activities is infinite, but we can put them all into two main categories: **(1) teacher led activities,** and **(2) students working independently of the teacher.**

The diagram opposite provides a simple classification of classroom activities. It does not claim to be exhaustive, but it will be the framework round which the following chapters in the book will be organised. The brief notes which follow are simply intended to define the various categories. Further description of techniques and styles will be given in later chapters.

Teacher Led Activities

Whole Class

The best known of teaching arrangements, often referred to as *traditional* teaching. But it must not be despised or rejected. When it is well done it can be very powerful.

Teacher Presentation can be very effective, provided it is used sparingly, for very short periods, and with sparkle. We must not deny our young people the experience of being inspired and stimulated by the charisma of a really good presenter. And, happily, many teachers can provide just that.

Class Dialogue or the so-called 'Socratic' method is a very useful method. The teacher leads the thinking of the class by skilful questioning. It is very commonly used, and at its best it can be lively and motivating for the students. It needs careful handling, however; it can so easily lose its vitality and become somewhat mechanical and repetitive.

Student Activities are important. Most teachers recognise that giving the students 'something to do' helps to bring variety into whole class

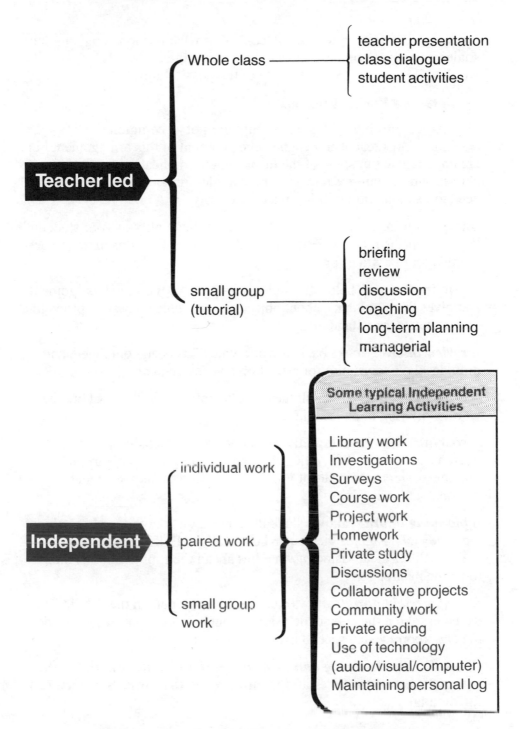

Teacher led

Whole class
- teacher presentation
- class dialogue
- student activities

small group
(tutorial)
- briefing
- review
- discussion
- coaching
- long-term planning
- managerial

Independent

individual work

paired work

small group
work

Some typical Independent Learning Activities

Library work
Investigations
Surveys
Course work
Project work
Homework
Private study
Discussions
Collaborative projects
Community work
Private reading
Use of technology
(audio/visual/computer)
Maintaining personal log

The Components of Classroom Management

teaching. The teacher remains in control of what is happening, but the students are given opportunities to be much more active. It is worthwhile making a serious study of the possibilities.

Small Group Work (Tutorials)

Teacher led tutorials with small groups are not as common as class teaching. Most teachers recognise the potential of this arrangement but are uncertain about some of the management implications with large classes and immature students. These are legitimate doubts and we shall need to examine possibilities in a careful way.

But if you want to make a real difference to the quality of your students' learning, this is the way forward. So developments in this direction are worth a lot of extra effort.

A briefing tutorial helps the students prepare for their next assignment, and gives them guidance about objectives, resources, possible problems, opportunities, and standards.

A review tutorial looks back at work which has been completed, and provides the opportunity for reflection and assessment.

A discussion tutorial encourages the students to talk freely about the work, exploring issues and ideas together.

A coaching tutorial allows the teacher to work intensively to help overcome students' difficulties. With the small group it becomes possible to get to the heart of problems and to offer support which is personal and individualised.

A planning tutorial allows students to participate in the thinking about the pace and design of the course being followed. If they share with their teacher a clear vision of what lies ahead their motivation is likely to be much stronger.

A managerial tutorial allows students to participate in the detailed decisions about the course, decisions about resources, contacts outside the classroom, visits, special events, and so on.

(Book 4 of the *Teaching and Learning Series* examines in detail the rationale, contexts, styles and techniques of Tutoring. See page 124 for details)

Independent Activities

Students will thrive if they are given a reasonable degree of independence. They need the teacher's guidance and help, of course, but they also need their own time and space, and sufficient decision making of their own. A wise teacher aims to strike a balance in order to get just the right amount of independence for each individual student.

Just as in class teaching there is a danger of monotony. Simply getting students to work on their own is no guarantee of high levels of motivation. There is still a lot of truth in the old jibe - *Death by a thousand worksheets!*

Individual Work

The opportunity to work entirely alone should be given frequently to all students. Some kinds of work lend themselves particularly well to this arrangement. Of course, good prior briefing is essential, as is the need to give additional support if it is required.

Paired Work

This is very popular and needs encouragement. Friendship is normally the best basis for the pairing. It is quite easy to use the pair as the normal unit for independent work and to break for individual work occasionally, or combine with other pairs for small group work.

Small Group Work

At its best this is very productive. It is not easy, however. Left to their own devices many young students run into difficulties and a lot of care is needed on the part of the teacher. **It is important to remember that working skilfully as a member of a small group is a fairly advanced activity - many adults can't do it!** So the teacher is wise to regard the independent small group as a training ground, and to monitor progress very carefully.

Typical Activities

These will not be described since the names given on the diagram are more or less self-explanatory. Later chapters will expand this list and discuss some of these activities in much more detail.

B Design

With such a variety of activities to choose from and the desire to offer variety to the students, how are the decisions made? Is it a question of simply *ringing the changes* to relieve possible monotony? Or is a deliberately planned approach likely to be more effective? The latter, surely.

It is a question of deciding where each kind of activity can make the most useful contribution. Some topics and needs are best met by class teaching, others by independent work. Some are best handled by the whole class, and others by individuals or small groups. The style of the good classroom manager is that of *contingency management* - making the methods fit the needs of the situation. **The good classroom manager is not the slave of any system or method.**

The diagram below suggests an outline design for the teaching of a topic.

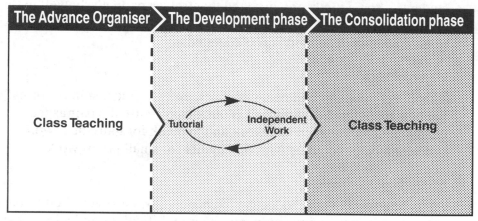

The Advance Organiser	The Development phase	The Consolidation phase
Class Teaching	Tutorial Independent Work	Class Teaching

An Outline Design

The Advance Organiser

When a new topic is being introduced the students need a great deal of help. Their needs are both intellectual and personal.

They need to have a vision of the new knowledge:

- why is it important and relevant?

- how does it fit in with our previous work?
- how will it contribute to mastery of the subject as a whole?
- what are the main ideas of this topic?

They also need to be inspired by the prospect of the new knowledge:

- to be helped to identify personally with it
- to have had access to clear 'images' of what the topic is about
- to have shared the excitement of the discovery of the knowledge
- to have a sense of sharing an experience with fellow students.

This is the advance organiser. It is, without doubt, the occasion for charismatic whole class teaching. The term *lead lesson* has often been used to describe this occasion, and in the literature of team teaching it was assumed that this would be delivered to a larger group than the conventional class and that it would be made into a very special event by the use of technology and very thorough preparation.

One such lesson, however, is not likely to be sufficient. It may be better to think of the advance organiser phase as taking up several class lessons. The first might be of the *lead lesson* type, but gradually the students would become much more involved as they move nearer to the next phase.

The Development Phase

Good class teaching needs to be followed up by well-organised independent work backed by support in small groups. A detailed discussion of the techniques and styles of this phase will be deferred until a later chapter, but some general points may be helpful now.

☐ There will need to be a simple *starter* mechanism to get the two-stroke engine working. This can most easily be accomplished by gradually introducing independent work during the class teaching phase.

☐ The students will almost certainly complete several cycles of this phase: tutorial - independent work - tutorial - independent work - and so on.

☐ Considerable attention will have had to be given to resources in preparation for this phase.

☐ In the early stages of working this way teachers may prefer to brief the students for their independent work as a whole class.

This is easier to do, and it provides a useful first step for both teacher and students. But it shouldn't prevent a march forward into the more difficult, but potentially more powerful, small group tutorial system.

The Consolidation Phase

After a period of time working individually, in pairs or in small groups, the students will be ready to come back together as a whole class.

The style of the consolidation phase needs to be different from the advance organiser phase. Instead of relying on high quality teacher presentation, much more attention should now be paid to the contributions that the students themselves can make. It is a time for *reporting back, discussion* of issues raised, *revising* and *consolidating, assessing* the quality of the work done, and *evaluating* the whole topic.

So there will be heavy use of student activities organised on a class basis.

C Variations in Design

The outline design described above will serve well in a large number of situations. Yet there is nothing immutable about it. Two possible variations are now suggested, and teachers, no doubt, will find many more.

1) Introduce the topic by getting the students to carry out a simple piece of preliminary research. Make arrangements for them to report back, and then give the class lessons of the advance organiser.

2) Divide the topic into two (or even three) parts in order to have more consolidation time. The sequence would be: advance organiser - independent work - consolidation - independent work - consolidation.

D Conclusion

This chapter has served as our advance organiser for the rest of the book. It has given an outline of the possibilities. We now need to examine the detail of the various methods and techniques.

Preparing The Classroom

PREPARING THE CLASSROOM

In this chapter we consider the classroom itself - the space, the furniture, the fittings, the equipment and the layout of all of these.

Of course it is not possible to deal with all the different situations in which teachers will be working. Many subjects require special equipment and layout, and individual rooms vary greatly in shape and size.

However it is hoped that some of the principles discussed will spark off debate as to how the work spaces themselves can be adapted to help in the moves towards better classroom management.

A ### The Organisation of Space

The Storage Problem

We need space for two main purposes - **work** and **storage.** It is surprising how frequently the storage needs of the classroom are allowed to put pressure on the work space needs.

Consider the traditional layout of many small classrooms. For example, in the diagram below it is clear that the amount of work space is inadequate.

The 'Desks in Rows' Layout

The students are packed tightly in the middle of the room and the scope
for flexible working is severely restricted. No wonder that teachers
working in such classrooms prefer the students to remain in their places!
The trouble is that the teacher's legitimate need for storage space has
been allowed to take priority over the students' need for work space.

This is a serious problem. Not only is flexible working made difficult,
but the room has a disturbing influence on motivation and attitudes.
There is a loss of dignity and an increase in petty irritations. What can
be done? Consider the following suggestions:

Store in the classroom only those resources that are in current use
Admittedly this is a counsel of perfection. But it is an end that is worth
striving for. Teachers who adopt this idea find that they prefer to store
resources on trolleys so that the resources can be wheeled into the
classroom when they are required and wheeled out again when they are
not needed. Some organisation is needed, both in setting up the system
and in operating it, but students can take on some of the responsibility.

Find space for those long term storage outside the classroom
You may be blessed with a large purpose-built store room or cupboard
fairly near at hand. If so, consider how it may be best used. If not you
must find space. Consider the following possibilities, bearing safety
regulations in mind:

- convert a spare cloakroom bay into additional storage space
- build high-level shelving above cloak racks for the storage of
  bulky materials not immediately needed
- move any slim, lockable cupboards just outside the classroom
  door.

Find space outside the classroom to serve as additional work space
- if the corridor is wide enough, give it a table or bench which the
  students can use for noisy, dirty, or space-consuming activities
- convert unused cloakroom areas into extra work stations for
  independent work.

Alternative Classroom Layouts

Let us assume that we have been able to take some of the pressure off the classroom space in some of the ways described above. What alternatives are there to the traditional 'desks in rows' layout?

The 'Cabaret' Style

This is a splendid layout which helps the teacher to mix class teaching with student activities, either in pairs or small groups. The diagram below shows *teams* or *tables* of six students, but it works well with slightly larger or smaller groupings.

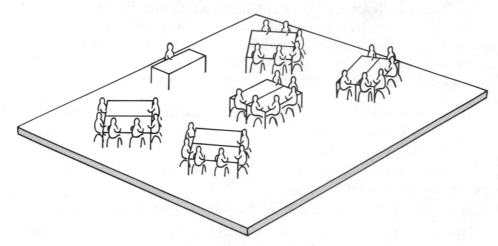

The 'Cabaret' Layout

We shall consider the detailed operations using this layout in a later chapter.

The 'Dining Room' Style

This focuses much more on small group activity. It can work well with students who are experienced in small group work, but it can cause problems:

- some students have their backs to the teacher which is slightly awkward during longer spells of class teaching
- during periods of individual work students are easily distracted by students sitting opposite.

The 'Dining Room' Layout

The 'Dining Room' style is frequently found in classrooms. It is often used for small group activity, but in many situations the students sitting around the table are not required to function as a group. When this happens the arrangement is often counter-productive.

The 'Workstations' Style

In this arrangement the classroom is designed like a modern open plan office. Like the modern office the classroom must provide for privacy as well as for group activity.

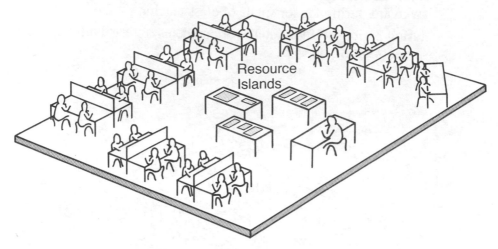

Resource
Islands

The 'Workstation' Layout

The diagram above demonstrates some of the advantages of this layout:

- it works quite well in class teaching; all the students can see the teacher and be seen
- all students can see the projection screen and blackboard
- because the resources are in the centre of the room all resource-seeking expeditions are short and direct, with the minimum of disturbance for others
- the furniture can serve well for individual study or paired work
- the furniture can be quickly adapted for small group work by removing partitions
- the large space in the centre of the room can be easily and quickly cleared for whole-class discussions, for drama, or for any practical activities requiring space.

These are substantial advantages and it is worth a lot of effort to achieve them. Of course, much trial and error is needed to determine the best layout for any given room. Cooperation is also required among all the users of a room. The principle of students on the periphery and the resources in the centre is well worth trying.

B ## Adaptations to Furniture

In many subject areas the furniture is specialised but where furniture is *general purpose* a lot can be accomplished.

The Students' Desks

We are assuming in our classroom that there will be a fair amount of individual or paired work. So it is worthwhile trying to improve the conditions for it. The purpose-built *carrel* or *study booth* springs to mind. This cuts out distractions and creates a private world which encourages concentration and thoughtful reflection. On the other hand it might be unwise to invest in expensive commercial products which would be heavy and inflexible in use. It is just as easy to have some simple partitions made from chipboard or lightweight fibreboard. A standard (8'x4') sheet will make two such partitions. For safety the edges of the board should be rounded and smoothed and some simple device will be needed to make sure that the board will not fall if the tables are moved. The advantage of the simple removable board is that the arrangement can be easily switched from the ideal conditions for paired work to one large table for small group work.

The Resources Area

In our workstation layout this would be in the centre of the room, but it could also be conveniently sited in one corner. Ideally it would only contain resources that were in current use. If space permits it is useful to think of several small specialist areas within the one room. This has the advantage of relieving congestion at busy times. Thus there might be in a central area several *resource islands*, each with its own distinctive purpose.

Trolleys are valuable since the resources can be easily taken out of the room when no longer in use. These can work out rather expensive and homemade purpose-built units using Dexion or similar materials can be effective and reasonably cheap.

C ## The Contents of the Resource Areas

These should contain a comprehensive collection of everything that the students are likely to need. The teacher's objective should be to have nothing to do with the organisation of the resources after the areas have been initially planned. Ambitious classrooms become very busy places with students requiring a large number of varied resources and tools. **It is fatal for classroom management when the teacher becomes addicted to helping students find what they need!** The teacher has

more important things to do. So careful planning and setting up are
essential.

Here is a check list for the resource areas. Of course, each teacher must
create a personal one based on subject and course needs. But this shows
the level of detailed planning necessary.

Resources Specific to the Current Unit of Study

- printed and non-print resources organised by a simple
  classification for easy retrieval
- assignment material, carefully housed and classified
- test material
- reference material - subject reference books, dictionaries,
  encyclopedias, etc.

General Resources

- A bank of stationery - ruled paper, plain paper, graph papers,
  tracing paper, blotting paper, coloured paper, scrap paper.
- A collection of writing and drawing tools - pens, pencils, rubbers,
  rulers, drawing instruments, scissors, adhesive tape, coloured
  pencils, pencil sharpeners, masking tape.
- Small equipment for individual or small group use - short throw
  slide / filmstrip projectors, slide / filmstrip viewers, audio-cassette
  players, personal computers. A mains cable fitted round the
  perimeter of the room with socket outlets just above desk top
  height can be a great help.

Finally, it is worth re-emphasising the importance of good organisation.
The richly resourced classroom is not necessarily the first step towards
good classroom management; it can so easily become the first step
towards chaos! There are a number of points to consider.

- Is the storage provided just the right size and so well labelled that
  materials can be found instantly?
- Can the collections of resources be checked easily and quickly
  when required, particularly at the end of lessons?
- Has a team of *monitors* been appointed and trained to carry out all
  the routine tasks that the resources system requires?
- Have all the students been shown the systems in operation and
  been given firm guidance on rules and procedures for using them?

Apply these two simple tests.

(1) How many times in the course of a lesson do students put questions about the location or availability of resources to the teacher?

(2) How much time during the course of the lesson does the teacher give to resources organisation?

The good classroom manager is a perfectionist in these matters and will aim to have a nil response to both questions.

D   The Teacher's Resources

It is not necessary to give detailed guidance about those resources which help the teacher to convey the message of a lesson in vivid and appealing ways. These resources are in such common use that considerable expertise is widespread. However, in the interests of giving a complete account of preparing the classroom, a few selected points are made about each of these commonly used items.

The Chalkboard

It would be a pity if good chalkboard techniques were allowed to die in the face of all the new technology now available. The chalkboard is instant and in capable hands it can be very powerful. So it is worthwhile to have lots of space available, and to practise the skills:

- intelligent and generous use of space
- bold and simple graphics
- coloured chalks
- designs which allow the students to add their own contributions.

The Overhead Projector

A good case can be made for the overhead projector. It has some distinct advantages:

- with a suitably mounted screen it can provide a very large image at a great height - no problems of students not being able to see!
- material (text, diagrams, maps) can be prepared in advance
- a range of sophisticated techniques can be used - use of coloured pens, shading and tinting, photocopying of well-designed material, use of several layers to build up an image or to reveal parts progressively
- it can be used like a chalkboard to develop an explanation, but with the teacher facing the class throughout.

Television with Video-recorder

The power of this combination is widely appreciated. In the hands of the best presenters it is frequently used as a serious source of raw data and stimuli rather than as a little light relief from teaching! So much use is made of the fast forward, rewind, pause and search facilities of the recorder, as well as the on-off switch! This principle is being extended in a most exciting way by the introduction of inter-active video.

Other Projected Visual Aids

Nowadays it is fairly common for the chalkboard to be supplemented by a variety of projected visual images. The requirements however need to be studied carefully; it is all too easy to spoil the effect of good material by poor attention to the technical details of the projection.

- Socket outlets are needed at the front of the room and at the back so that the needs of different pieces of equipment can be met.

- It should be possible to dim the room so that the best results can be obtained when required.

- Careful attention should be given to the screen - wide enough, high enough, angled against the main source of light, tilted for OHP, and with no student having to view at too acute an angle.

Audio Aids

The radio and the tape recorder, used separately or in combination, add another dimension to the teacher's repertoire. Sadly they are not always fully exploited, although their value is recognised as sources of stimulating experience which will help students improve their own listening and speaking skills.

E

Summary

☐ The classroom must serve for **teacher presentations, small-group work,** and for **individual study.** All this needs a lot of space. So it may be necessary to remove from the classroom all resources other than those in current use.

☐ Alternatives to the traditional layout of desks should be explored. The **cabaret** style, the **dining room** style, and the **workstation** style offer good prospects.

☐ **Furniture** can be adapted to support the versatility demanded of the classroom. Study booths which can quickly support individual, paired, small group, and whole class work can be made.

☐ The **resource** areas in the room should be comprehensive and thoroughly organised. The aim is to release the teacher from all resource management tasks.

(The whole question of resources is dealt with in more detail in Book 3 of the Teaching and Learning Series. See page 123 for more details)

Whole Class Teaching Exposition and Dialogue

The techniques of exposition

The techniques of class dialogue

WHOLE CLASS TEACHING : EXPOSITION AND DIALOGUE

We have already argued that whole class teaching plays an important part in good classroom management. Its great contribution is as an *advance organiser* and as a consolidator. This chapter examines what is often referred to as traditional class teaching. In this the teacher plays a leading role relying on high quality exposition and the building up of a dialogue between the teacher and the students.

The discussion of active learning within a class teaching mode is saved for the succeeding chapter.

Introduction

In traditional class teaching the teacher is the focus of attention, playing a number of related roles: *organiser; information giver; discussion leader.* The students are relatively passive (though not entirely so with a skilled teacher): *listening; following instructions; responding to questions; making contributions when invited to do so.*

Sadly, a lot of class teaching is dull and stifling. Critics claim that class teaching relies too much on teacher talk, that the students are not active in their own learning, that individual differences are ignored, that students are regimented in such a way as to create low motivation, poor performance, and unsatisfactory personal relationships. All this is true of class teaching at its worst, and when it is used as an exclusive method. No teacher, however dedicated, can be inspiring and stimulating for **every** lesson throughout a whole school year.

But it is a pity when the reaction against class teaching is so strong as to imply that it has no place in the repertoire of the good teacher. In Chapter One we have described the roles that class teaching can play in a comprehensive strategy of good classroom management. **When it is not the only method in use there is less of it; and less can mean better.** Good class teaching is a vital part of the repertoire, and we must explore its potential.

A The Techniques of Exposition

What is Exposition?

Exposition is the informing, describing, and explaining which is part of every teacher's stock in trade. But exposition in school is different from the set lecture which features so much in higher education. School exposition tends to be informal and spontaneous, and to be very short - probably not much more than 10 minutes with younger students. The exposition is invariably relieved by short bursts of other activity - a classroom dialogue, or some tasks to be done individually.

Why is it important?

But having put exposition firmly in its place as a brief and only occasional undertaking, we need now to sing its praises. It can be very attractive and very powerful. Young students still need the charisma of the good teacher. Good exposition can do all of these:

- motivate and inspire students
- stimulate their intellectual curiosity
- provide an advance organiser of new subject matter
- provide a supporting framework for a whole course of study
- review and consolidate
- make the new learning more personal through accounts which are based on first-hand knowledge
- give guidance to the students about the styles and techniques which are likely to be of most use in tackling new work.

When is it best used?

Exposition can take place at any time during a course of study, but it is particularly valuable at the beginning *(the advance organiser)*, at the end *(the consolidation phase)*, and at critical points such as topic changes or where the concepts are difficult.

What should be attempted in an Exposition?

If the exposition has a clear structure that the students can grasp it will stand a better chance of achieving its objectives. It helps greatly if students are invited at the very beginning to **share** with the teacher an understanding of the way that the exposition is going to unfold. Sometimes keeping them in the dark can be stimulating, but it can also be tiring and confusing. It is better to make the structure of the exposition explicit. The idea is similar to the advice often given to public speakers:

- first tell them what you are going to say
- then say it
- then tell them what you have said!

A good way of involving the students is to give them a handout which displays the structure of the forthcoming exposition and which requires some student contribution in order to complete it. A variation on this idea is to get the students to build up notes or a diagram on the chalkboard. This requires less preparation, but the students have nothing to take away from the lesson.

Examples of Exposition Structures

The Sequential Structure

In this exposition the teacher is simply explaining a sequence of events, or steps in a process, or a chain of causes and effects. The students' handout would have main headings and the teachers would pause at the end of each stage to allow a few notes or key words to be entered. Alternatively the handout could be a diagram in skeleton form which the student would be invited to complete while listening to the exposition.

The Deductive Structure

In this the teacher explains and justifies a set of rules or principles and then goes on to describe a number of examples or consequences derived from the principles. Again a handout would help, particularly if it allows opportunity for students to add the results of their own knowledge or thoughts.

The Inductive Structure

In this the teacher presents a number of examples or case studies and helps the students to arrive at generalisations or rules based on them. The exposition might have the following stages:

- briefly describe two examples or case studies
- students are invited to identify similarities and differences
- briefly describe a third example
- extend the discussion about similarities and differences
- tentatively establish principles, rules, or generalisations.

Within this process there are ample opportunities for the teacher to encourage students to examine their own thought processes and the ways in which conclusions are reached. Thus the exposition makes a contribution to the students' growing intellectual maturity.

The Problem-solving Structure

Students like problem-solving and they will join in with enthusiasm. The exposition could go through these stages:

- State the problem as clearly as possible
- Invite the students to conjecture a possible solution
- Get the students to help in finding plus points and minus points for the proposed solution
- Get them to make a decision. Is the proposed solution acceptable as it stands? Or does it need modifying? Or should it be rejected and a new solution sought?
- Continue the process with a search for clearer definition of the problem and a number of conjectures as to the likely solution.

Problem -solving is an excellent way for the students to appreciate the provisional nature of much of our knowledge. We can only produce solutions in the light of our existing knowledge and understanding.

The Compare and Contrast Structure

This is a well-tried approach in which the pupils can become engrossed in identifying similarities and differences between two sets of events, situations, or conditions. The material should be presented vividly and the use of structured notes regarded as essential.

The Subject Heading Structure

In the presentation of some topics students need to be given a lot of information. A clear structure with lots of headings and sub-headings can be very helpful to them. There is, however, a danger of such an exposition losing its sparkle. So every effort should be made to make the ideas attractive, and to give the students something to contribute in the building up of the framework.

What are the styles and techniques of good Exposition?

This is a matter of personal style and much of the technique of a good teacher is intuitive. However, techniques are worth analysing, on the understanding that the suggestions are not to be treated as rigid prescriptions for all people in all places at all times!

Get the attention of the class before you start

This can be done by a mixture of plain insistence and by giving them something to do. The latter may be little more than writing a title or an introductory statement, but it can help enormously to bring the class into the work frame of mind.

Your first sentences must be attention holding

Appeal to their curiosity; surprise them or intrigue them; move them emotionally. Of course, it can be overdone. So *sensitivity* is the order of the day. But it is the mark of a skilful teacher that these attention holding techniques can be used without alienating the students in any way. A serious and quiet sincerity can help a lot.

Keep your voice level to the minimum necessary

A low voice level creates a feeling of expectancy, gives a sense of importance to the occasion, and creates a mood of mutual confidence. It is surprising how many teachers are noisy in their classrooms. They hector their classes even when they are not quarrelling with them! **A quiet teacher makes a quiet class.** But even more important, a quiet teacher creates a serious and trusting atmosphere.

Vary the volume and pace to give variety

A **low** voice level is an excellent base on which to build some variations. To excite and stimulate the students, a different pace or a different volume is required. When students are concentrating well on the words of the teacher, a line of reasoning can be made more exciting by an **increased pace** of delivery; the student gets the feeling of rapid mastery of new knowledge and a sense of adventure in being able to stay with the argument.

On other occasions an appeal can be made to **feelings**, by a more theatrical use of language. Education is just as much about feelings as about thinking, and we should not be ashamed to express our own feelings. But these projections of the teacher's personality need to be tempered with sensitivity. Beware of over-indulgence, insincerity, and self-centred histrionics.

There is also the virtue of **silence.** The *pregnant pause* in an exposition can be effective. But sometimes silence should also be formally offered to the students so that they can reflect on weighty statements or significant problems, and consider their own responses.

Throughout the skilful teacher is able to consider the needs of the students without losing track of the development of the ideas in the exposition.

Make sure that the students never lose sight of the structure of the whole exposition.

We have already said - *Tell them what you are going to say. Say it. Then tell them what you have said.* It is the principle of reinforcement.

It is good too to have frequent pauses in which a student is invited to summarise the argument so far.

Take great care in the use of language

As teachers we have to accept that in some senses our own education and training have left us with handicaps. We are subject specialists, brought up in an academic tradition, heavy users of reading and writing, and having to deal more and more with the bureaucracies of central and local government. The words we choose to use are often more suitable for academic textbooks or government reports than for speaking to a group of young people. So we need to be on our guard when talking to our students. Look out for *pedantic* language, avoid *jargon* and the language of the bureaucrat; use concrete rather than *abstract* words and phrases. Beware of *verbosity* and be alert to overworked *metaphors* and *cliches.*

Teachers need to follow three basic principles: **be simple; be short; be human.** In pursuit of these principles it is better to choose:

- the concrete noun rather than the abstract
- the active voice rather than the passive
- the short sentence rather than the long
- the simple sentence rather than the compound
- the direct statement rather than the circumlocution
- people as the subject wherever possible.

When introducing an abstract concept it is better to start with plenty of concrete examples, which are within the experience of the students. These examples provide temporary props for the new concept. Then gradually the teacher can introduce new vocabulary and more complex statements.

Remember that much communication between teacher and students is non-verbal

How you **look**, where and how you **stand**, how you **move** are all observed and registered by the students. Certainly distracting habits need to be eliminated, and the confident teacher will find out from the students what these are.

But non-verbal communication is an important asset in good exposition. It can help improve the students' concentration and get more sympathetic responses. Communication by example, by signal, by gesture should all be practised. The effective communicator can often achieve a lot without uttering a word.

B   The Techniques of Class Dialogue

Pure exposition is not normally used for lengthy periods in the classroom for younger students. Teachers know that their span of attention has strict limits, and it is better to introduce variety with more student participation. The most common way of doing this is by setting up a class dialogue. In this the teacher leads the thinking of the class by asking questions and building on the responses received from the students. It is sometimes given the name *Socratic Questioning*. At its best it can stimulate and produce high-level thinking; at its worst it can be pedestrian and stifling. So it is worth analysing the opportunities and the possible pitfalls.

Preparation

Although class dialogue is an interactive form of learning, it does benefit from careful preparation. The teacher needs to have a mental picture of the intended build-up of knowledge and understanding. This build-up might start with familiar, concrete examples in order to establish some simple concepts. Then the questions can gradually move into unfamiliar territory, towards more advanced concepts and abstract ideas. It is the lack of preparation that leads to opening questions like:

This lesson is about the Boer War. Who can tell me what they know about the Boer War?'

The likely response is a withering silence, but even if the teacher is lucky and gets an interesting response to build on, it would have been safer to have phased the introduction of the topic more carefully.

The planned phases of a class dialogue might look something like this.

1 Stimulus	The teacher presents a stimulus: a picture; a map; a drawing; a piece of text; a short exposition; a sound or video recording. The aim is to rouse curiosity in order to start the questioning.	
2 Development	The teacher's questions help students to build upon their existing knowledge and understanding.	
3 Generalisation	The teacher helps the students to recognise general statements and principles from their new found knowledge.	

4 Performance and Feedback	The questions now are designed to give the students opportunities to demonstrate their understanding. They are tested on their knowledge and invited to apply it .

The Questions

It is hard to prepare the exact wording of the questions in advance, and this is probably not desirable, since the questions need to be adapted to the responses being received. There are however a number of general questioning skills which can be cultivated.

The language must be simple, clear and unambiguous

The questioning should start with an invitation to observe or identify

The key word is **'What?'** Here are some examples:

- *What are the people in this picture doing?*
- *What is the difference between these two shapes?*
- *What surprised you in this brief description?*
- *What is this?*

The questions should encourage the students to give extended answers

Consider how it might be possible to eliminate questions which can be answered simply by *Yes* or *No*, or by any single word. *What?, When?, Where?* questions tend to get one word answers. *Do you?* and *Don't you?* tend to get *Yes* or *No*.

Questions likely to get fuller answers often start with *Why....?, How....?*, or *What would happen if....?*

The questions should build up to higher levels of thinking

The careful use of *How?* and *Why?* and *What would happen if?* questions can lead to students achieving these desirable goals:

- using evidence to come to conclusions
- applying rules and principles to specific instances
- solving problems
- using imagination
- formulating and testing hypotheses
- evaluation.

The Students' Responses

Getting the best responses from the students calls for patience and skill. If we are ambitious for them we are making very big demands on ourselves. Here are some suggestions:

Be prepared to wait for an answer

If the question is greeted with initial silence there is a natural tendency to fill the gap. This soon leads to teacher domination of the proceedings and students find it comfortable to allow the teacher to provide the answers. During the silence use opportunities for non-verbal communication. Look for the student who is on the brink of a contribution - an encouraging nod or a raised eyebrow can often tip the balance. Or try a very short prompt which will encourage the faint-hearted. Sometimes, with the right group, playing *devil's advocate* will relax the tension and provoke a response. But beware of saying too much! Above all it is vital to signal that you are actually enjoying the silence and are not in the least embarrassed, still less annoyed.

Encourage their contributions

Praise the good answers. Use the names of those who have a go. Preserve the **self-esteem**[1] of those who give wrong answers by taking their answers seriously and by rewarding them with praise or a friendly gesture. Give help if it is needed during an answer. Sometimes a single word prompt, or a helpful re-phrasing, even just a nod, will encourage a student to press on. The skill is to know when to withdraw.

Try to get contributions from as many students as possible.

Responding only to the raised hands of the bright and eager tends to focus attention on them at the expense of all the others. So while they must be allowed their fair share, opportunity must be found to get some of the others active. A particularly reluctant student can be helped by being nominated to answer an easy question before the question is asked.

Encourage the response which expresses the personal thoughts or feelings of the student

The classroom is a very public place and as such thoughtfulness and sensitivity often get a poor deal. A quiet and serious style helps the

---

[1]   The question of self-esteem is dealt with in more detail in Book 3 of the series, *Resources for Flexible Learning.*

teacher overcome this, particularly if the teacher also has the confidence to demonstrate personally the thoughtful reflection and sensitive response as an example for the students.

Encourage the response which is bold and imaginative

Even if it is incorrect, such a response must be given praise. Intellectual boldness and imagination should be given status in the classroom, and it is worth devoting time to encouraging it.

Encourage respect for the contribution of others

Set a good example of courtesy, respect and constructiveness. Then expect it of the students. Do not tolerate sarcasm, mockery, aggression, or destructive criticism.

Discussion Techniques

Effective questioning naturally leads into class discussion. There is no clear boundary between the two. However, it has to be conceded that the average class is far too big to operate as a successful discussion group. So class discussion is best thought of as a variant of teacher questioning.

So the teacher should expect to be in firm control. The rules for the discussion should be clearly established and the rules of procedure laid down.

Once the housekeeping has been properly arranged, the teacher, in the role of discussion leader, needs to exercise a *democratic* rather than an *authoritarian* style. All the techniques of skilful questioning need to be used with the additional skill of withdrawal into *neutrality.* Student contributions must be encouraged with reinforcement, prompting, and occasional summaries as to where the discussion has reached.

It is wise to set a strict time limit to a discussion and to bring it to a satisfactory close by summarising the main points made and conclusions reached. Discussion techniques are particularly useful for objectives concerned with personal attitudes, and for those concerned with problem solving.

4

Whole Class Teaching
Active Learning

Setting the scene for active learning
The techniques of active learning

WHOLE CLASS TEACHING : ACTIVE LEARNING

There is no reason why whole class teaching should be regarded as exclusively didactic. Students can learn in *active* ways when they are working as a whole class.

We need active learning within whole class teaching, not only for the variety it brings.

☐   Active learning gives young students a valuable training; they are learning to make the decisions of the responsible learner, but always under the supervision and guidance of the teacher.

☐   Active learning offers the best way of moving a programme of work from the didactic towards the more independent styles. It is a perfect tool for making what could be a difficult transition.

Most teachers make considerable use of active methods during whole class teaching. Their interest in active methods is more likely to be concerned with improvement rather than with an entirely new set of techniques.

A

Setting the Scene for Active Learning

Active learning techniques can be easily introduced without any special preparations, but there are some distinct advantages in thinking ahead about things like *classroom layout* and *group dynamics*.

Classroom layout

We have already argued the weaknesses of the traditional *desks in rows* arrangement of furniture. These become even more apparent when active learning techniques are being tried. Active learning thrives best with:

• plenty of space so that activities other than reading, writing and listening can be considered

• a flexible layout so that the students can, when required, collaborate with each other either as members of a small group or simply in a pair

• a layout which can also allow the teacher to direct the activities of the whole class, and when necessary, revert to short sessions of exposition or class dialogue.

These conditions are not met where the traditional layout is used. In order to illustrate the possibilities for active learning with the whole

class we shall use the *cabaret style* of layout described in Chapter 2.
This does a much better job than the *desks in rows*. In the *cabaret* the
students all face the teacher, and exposition and class dialogue can be
easily done. But the grouping of the students means that the whole class
can switch instantly into the very short sessions of group collaboration
that this method requires.

The Role of the Team in Active Learning

In the *cabaret* layout the class is organised into teams. The members of
each team share a common table but sit only on three sides of the table
so that they can easily attend to the teacher at the front of the class.

The Size of the Team

What is the optimum size of a team? As the table shows we are trying
to strike a balance.

	Large Team	**Small Team**
Level of student participation	Each student only gets a small share of the action	Each student gets a bigger share of the action
Range of opinions and responses brought to the discussions	Varied and therefore stimulating	Probably inadequate

The best balance is probably achieved with teams in the range 4 to 8
students. The team is large enough to produce a variety of opinions and
responses, and yet small enough to give each student a sense of
belonging.

It is an advantage if each team consists of an even number of students (4
or 6 are most likely, but 8 is possible). This allows the teacher the
option of setting activities for pairs or for the whole team. In fact, a
common approach will be to start an activity with paired work and then
take the results or conclusions to the whole group.

Generally speaking it is a good principle to keep the number of teams
down to the minimum possible. For example, a class of 30 students
would only require 5 teams if the team size was 6.

The Composition of the Team

It is difficult to establish general rules. Much depends on the age and experience of the students, the spread of subject ability within the class, and the subject matter being taught. However, a few general points can be made.

- Attempts at rigid streaming will have a particularly adverse effect on the least able team; it will present the teacher with an uphill task. A broader grouping by ability with a fair amount of overlapping should work better.

- There is a lot to be said for letting friendship play at least some part in the formation of the team. A good way is to start by inviting the students to choose partners for paired work, and then to form the teams from the pairs.

- Normally it is better if a team is of mixed gender. There may however be circumstances where single sex teams seem more helpful.

- In some instances it may be wise to allow the shy and retiring students to form a team of their own. They will not be submerged by the more vociferous members of the class and will be encouraged to take on responsibility within the team.

But, it is worth repeating, **there are no universal rules** and teachers should make their own decisions according to the logic of their own situations.

The Functions of the Team

When the teams are operating the teacher can now switch easily between exposition, class dialogue, paired work, and small group work. The activity of the team can become an important feature of the classroom work. No longer does the teacher have to keep the attention of all the students all the time. Teacher input can be sensibly punctuated by requests to the teams to consider their responses to questions. This is much easier than the traditional form of class dialogue, and it also has the virtue of giving every student the opportunity to participate, but without having to *go public* every time a contribution is made.

But the teams will be effective only if some ground work has been done. The identity and importance of each team must be firmly established. We are talking about *pride, loyalty, mutual support* and the *determination* to succeed. So we are faced with a need for some **team building**.

It would be unwise to regard this team building as a *one-off* exercise, to be attended to before the serious work starts. Developing these inter-personal skills requires persistence and a certain amount of opportunism. Some things will obviously need to be attended to at the outset, but thereafter the training will be *ad hoc*; it is learning on the job. Consider these suggestions for team building:

☐ *Give the team a short life-span.* Careful thought should be given to the life-span of the team. It is obviously not wise to keep chopping and changing, but permanent teams may not be the best solution. It is worth trying a short life span just to serve a specific part of a programme of study. So the team starts with a clearly defined task to be tackled within a defined time; this helps build the sense of team identity and removes the feeling of being locked indefinitely into a grouping which an individual may, for one reason or the other, find uncomfortable.

☐ *Give every team member a job.* Every member should have a *job* and be answerable to the team. There might be a **chairperson** *(decides agenda and keeps order during discussion)*, a **secretary** *(writes down decisions or information)*, a **spokesperson** *(speaks on behalf of the team)*, a **resources officer** *(makes sure that team members have the resources they need)*, a **record keeper** *(keeps records of achievements - both for individuals and for the whole team)*. Of course, different subjects may need different jobs; the examples given are simply for illustration. The jobs should be rotated fairly frequently.

☐ *Emphasise that they are there to help each other.* Every member of the team should know that help for another member of the team is not only allowed, it is actively encouraged. That is what the teams are for.

☐ *Recognise the team's successes.* With the previous principle in mind, the achievements of members of the team could be publicised and recorded not individually, but as sum totals for the team (like the old systems of *house points*!). Perhaps this can't operate all the time, but it should be used whenever possible.

☐ *Reward them as a team.* Rewards, *perks*, and light relief should be given on a team basis; likewise any minor sanctions!

□ *Train them as a team.*   Take every opportunity to *train* them in their roles and responsibilities as team members. It will yield dividends.

□ *Lead them towards self-management.*   With a sensible eye on what can be reasonably expected of the team in terms of their age and experience encourage them to take responsibility for their own team building. Let them move along the road towards *the self-managing team.*

Finding a Place for Active Learning

There are many ways in which active learning can be absorbed into a programme of work.   A most common sequence is as follows:

Exposition
To introduce a new topic

↓

Class Dialogue
To reinforce and practise the new ideas

↓

Active Learning Techniques
To give further practice particularly in the application of the new ideas

↓

Class Dialogue
To recapitulate and summarise

But the real benefit of a *cabaret* layout is that **the teacher can switch quickly from one mode to another.** Opportunities during class lessons are so varied that it would be wrong to imply that any one sequence is better than any other. On one day a class may be happy with a more extended exposition and a small amount of class dialogue. On another day, or with another topic, it might pay to get them quickly into team activity in order to keep them alert and involved. The skilful teacher uses flair, not a set of mechanical prescriptions.

The benefit of the team approach soon become apparent. Questions directed at the pairs or at the teams can anticipate longer, more thoughtful answers, the result of deliberation. This overcomes the main weakness of the class dialogue which can so easily degenerate into a kind of rapid fire - a succession of short questions, with one-word answers supplied by the bright and eager, and the teacher jumping from one student to another in search of the *right* answer. In the team approach everyone can take part, different solutions can be explored, and students learn to justify their arguments to their fellow team members.

B   The Techniques of Active Learning

So there can be no set sequence for the techniques of active learning. The teacher uses them according to a judgement about the way that the lesson is progressing.

Most of the techniques described below are small scale, and many of them are well-known. However it is useful to build up a repertoire as a check list so that a wide range can be used. The list of suggestions given here should be used as a basis for making a larger, more personal check list. Of course, a teacher will use more than one technique at a time. Many of them are complementary to each other.

Snowball	Let the first thinking about an issue or problem be done by individuals (perhaps resulting in a few rough notes). Then each student shares that thinking with the student's partner. Finally each pair reports to the team in order (if possible) to arrive at a team decision.
Flip Chart	Whenever teams are asked to consider a problem or issue, invite them each to enter one word only on the flip chart (or chalkboard) which neatly summarises their proposed solution. When all teams have entered their word, each team is invited to explain what its chosen word is intended to convey. An alternative is to let the teams contribute to the building up of patterned notes on the flip chart.
Handouts	Handouts are always useful. But they mustn't do all the work for the students. So leave something for the students to do - notes, labels, completion. Often simply providing headings and spaces in which to write or draw is all that is needed. Give them time to *do their bit*. Encourage them to discuss what they are doing with each other.

Library Copies

Make sure that the library has a copy of anything that you consider is important in the programme of study. For example, your important introduction to a topic could have been taped and a copy placed in the library together with any illustrations which may have been used. Encourage the students to use this facility. *(Note: simply tape your exposition as it occurs; they will accept it as such without elaborate editing.)*

Review

It is often helpful to start a lesson with a quick review of what happened in the last lesson. But make this the first job, on arrival, of the teams themselves. One team only will be selected to give the review, but all will have to prepare it, just in case they are asked!

Key Points

Towards the end of each lesson and at the end of each topic focus the attention of the class on the key points. Use active learning techniques. For example, invite each team to determine what they think have been the (say) four key points of a lesson. Then reveal your answers (dramatically!). Identify the best team solution and let them all reflect on the differences and similarities between theirs and yours.

Rough Paper or Book

Give them time to prepare their responses to questions or problems and to make notes in readiness for their pair or team discussion. See below under *Silence*.

Peer Coaching

When there are some issues or points that need understanding get the teams to tackle them through peer coaching. Define as accurately as you can the standard required and challenge each team to bring all its members up to that standard by mutual help. Invite them to indicate when they think they have reached the standard.

Team Teaching

For the purposes of an introductory exposition combine two classes and share the exposition with a colleague. Later invite your teams to try to identify differences in subject interest between the two teachers. (See below under *Disagreement*)

Student Questions   Student questions are more important than teachers' questions. So train them to ask good questions. They need time to formulate them (see *Silence* and *Rough Paper*). When each student has a question they could work in pairs to try to answer each other's question. Teams could subsequently decide and report the most interesting question that has been raised within the team.

Disagreement   Always emphasise that disagreement is interesting, and not an excuse for quarrelling. So when a problem is being discussed by a team, set them the task to define clearly the differences between their individual perceptions. When they have done that then they can report their preferred solution.

Silence   Frequently insist on silence so that everyone can quietly reflect. It gives students the opportunity to complete notes, look back over the work, prepare questions, etc.

Testing   Finish a lesson with a short test on the material covered in the lesson. As this will be for reinforcement rather than permanent assessment, make it into a team competition.
No mutual help allowed but the results are team totals, not individual.

Circle   This device does not use the team organisation. Clear the middle of the room so that all the students can sit in one big circle. A very friendly arrangement and excellent for general discussion and evaluation at the end of a topic.

Breaks   Don't be afraid of giving breaks, especially during long and difficult sessions.

Obviously the list could be expanded a great deal. But the ideas for this list should be kept to those that allow paired or team activity for very short periods of time within a lesson that is controlled by the teacher.

They are designed to make class teaching more inter-active. The more sustained group activities should be kept for a separate list.

This has been an important chapter because it is about the *link* between a *teacher dominated* classroom and a *student-centred* one. Getting the students to learn how to respond as a team to small problems and issues is the first step towards independent work and ultimate autonomy as learners. Operating in this way classroom life becomes much more friendly.

5

Towards Independent Learning

Collecting and organising resources

The Steps towards independent learning

Supervised Study

TOWARDS INDEPENDENT LEARNING

Most of us share a vision of the truly *autonomous learner* - a person who is highly motivated, thoroughly organised, and capable of making rational and responsible decisions about the use of resources and people and facilities for learning.

Most of us also recognise that our students aren't like that!

So we think of our work as giving them a *progressive training* towards the ultimate goal of autonomy. But we have to start where our students are now.

This chapter identifies the steps by which this progressive training might be given. The steps are described in a logical order, but it is not necessary to adhere strictly to that order. Training of this kind is opportunist; the skilled teacher will adapt to the students and to the topics being studied. But always this will be training on the job. The students will learn how to learn by being involved in real learning tasks. The demands which are made on their maturity and responsibility will grow as they become more capable.

A ## Collecting and Organising the Learning Resources

A separate book in this series has been entirely devoted to learning resources and readers are invited to study it for greater detail than is offered here. (See page 123 for details.) However, from the point of view of classroom management, there are some important principles. These are set out as firm statements, with a brief justification for each.

Don't assume that independent learning requires specially designed resources

This is not to deny that more and better resources can considerably enhance the quality of the students' experiences in school. But teachers would be mistaken if they believed that no progress can be made towards independent learning without new resources being bought or locally produced. The best advice to those about to embark on independent learning programmes is to start with the resources that you are already familiar with, and only think about expanding them when the system is running well.

Provide a good coursebook for the student working independently

A student who is asked to work independently even for short periods will benefit from a good coursebook. Such a book would be concise, well-structured, comprehensive, and reliable. It would provide the student with a secure framework - a prop in the absence of the teacher.

Put the student in contact with a wide variety of enrichment resources

It is quite wrong to force the independent learner into a narrow 'programmed learning' mode in which all stimulus comes from the one package, however carefully it has been designed. Independent work is linked closely with the intelligent use of libraries and other information sources.

Help the student with good assignment material

This is guidance which may have been prepared by the teacher in writing or on tape. It helps with information about resources, and with guidance on strategies and presentation. Sometimes short assignments are called worksheets or task cards.

Prefer resources that are available in small format

Within a classroom where independent learning is being developed the small topic booklet, the single sheet of data, the single illustration, the short audio-tape or filmstrip come into their own. They are an economical use of resources and can be sharply focused on the learning tasks.

Normally prefer to buy or borrow resources rather than to make them

It can be so time consuming, and, even with the improved technology available in school, it is likely to compare poorly with what the commercial publisher can produce. The usual exceptions to this general principle are assignments, local material, and material for which there is absolutely nothing available commercially.

Consider small sets of resources, rather than class sets

Class sets are sometimes required, but only where an item is likely to be in constant use by the whole class. For individual and small group work the small set works better and it is a much more economical system of buying.

Always explore the vast resources which exist outside the classroom and outside the school

Quite apart from the quantity and the quality of what is available there is an invaluable experience for the students in finding and using such resources.

Be systematic in the storage of the resources

Resources are there to be used and within the classroom a student must be able to find what is required. Elaborate classification and retrieval systems may not be the best solution. Regard the building up of a good resources base as a long-term commitment.

B

The Steps towards Independent Learning

Resources by themselves do not produce independent learning. We need to look at what actually happens in the classroom.

In making progress towards independent learning there are three variables to consider:

- the grouping in which the students work (individual, pair or small group)
- the way in which they are prepared and briefed for tasks
- the ways in which the teacher controls and monitors their progress.

Here are four possible steps by which a teacher might take a class on their road to greater independence and responsibility.

Step	Student Grouping	Briefing for Task	Monitoring and Control
1 Active Learning	Team	Whole class	Teacher directing whole class
2 Supervised Study	Individual or paired	Whole class	Teacher circulating
3 Supported Independent Work	Individual paired or small group	Tutorial group	Tutorials and teacher circulating
4 Self-Managing Teams	Individual, paired or small group	Negotiation with tutorial group	Mainly by tutorials

As you can see, the teacher starts with the whole class active learning which was described in the last chapter and then adjusts the variables to give the students greater responsibility.

The remainder of this chapter will be devoted to Step 2: *Supervised Study*. Steps 3 and 4 will be then be tackled in the two following chapters.

C The Next Step: Supervised Study

A Well-known Scenario

Supervised study is widely practised. Most teachers will recognise this scenario. The teacher has recognised that young students do not thrive if they have to sit still and listen to expositions all day long. Furthermore, the teacher has also recognised that there are limits to their span of attention within a class dialogue. The need to give them *something* to do is obvious.

So, arising out of the work that has been done so far, the teacher sets a task or a series of tasks to be done individually, or in pairs. The explanation of what to do and how to do it is given to the class as a whole. For the most part the teacher makes the decisions, but this doesn't have to be so and the teacher's ideas are often supplemented by suggestions from the students themselves.

The individuals or pairs then proceed with their tasks and the role of the teacher is monitorial - moving round the class, checking that everyone is on task, helping with problems, making suggestions, giving advice, and at the same time generally supervising work and conduct.

This simple system is widely practised in our schools. It has a number of strengths. It helps the students to be more active and it could be the start of a strong move towards real independence for the learners. Students generally like it and the teacher finds opportunity to talk to individuals or small groups, which is a welcome change from always addressing the whole class.

But there is a weakness if the system is allowed to become exclusive. Students are for the most part working individually and they could be deprived of the stimulus of working with other people. There is also an important danger. It is that the system could so easily become stuck at this point with the learners still dependent on the teacher's directions. Although they may be active they are not really involved in much decision making. So we need to examine this system critically, to find out what are the factors which prevent it developing.

The most common cause of the supervised study system getting stuck is, paradoxically, **the teacher's own desire to be helpful to the students.** We naturally want to feel that we are doing some good and so we are quick to respond to each and every request for help and advice as it comes. Without realising it we are sending messages to our students that asking the teacher for help is what we expect. Then the pressure of requests builds up and we find the system is quite exhausting, but we justify the expenditure of our effort on the grounds that this is the *changing role of the teacher.* In extreme cases this state of affairs reaches a point where the teacher is working harder than any other person in the room, and:

- has no time of his/her own because all the time is taken up by matters of importance to individual students
- is under such pressure that answers to questions are given hurriedly and briefly, and sustained dialogue is discouraged
- begins to lose track of what is happening generally
- starts neglecting some of the important things like student assessment and evaluation.

Some teachers on reaching this point abandon the system altogether saying that *it* doesn't work. And who can blame them! On the other hand it might be better to tackle this *mother hen* syndrome head on.

Overcoming the Weaknesses

In order to do so we may have, at least at the beginning, to suppress some of our instincts! We must recognise that bustling activity by the teacher is not a reliable indicator of student learning. In fact there is likely to be more hope in the *very opposite,* where the teacher is not under pressure and has some *discretionary time* available.

Let us work on this concept of *discretionary time.* Let us assume that if the teacher has more discretionary time during a lesson, it should be possible to use that time with greater effect. And it will also mean that the students are beginning to take on greater responsibility.

If this assumption is accepted we are left with the inescapable conclusion that there is a need to *cut down the number of student questions*! At first this may seem an outrageous assertion and it clearly needs justifying. But if we analyse the questions that the students ask we may begin to see possibilities. Because the questions we need to cut out are the unnecessary ones! And there are often plenty of those. But we must approach this with sensitivity and offer stimulating and acceptable alternatives to the students. Consider these suggestions as ways of doing just that.

Make sure that the initial briefing for a task has been thorough

Has enough time been given to it? Has it been explained clearly in sufficient detail? Have students been asked to summarise the main points to show that they have understood? Has time been given for questions about uncertainties or possible problems? The objective of each briefing must be that the students go away from it absolutely clear about what they have to do, where the resources are to be obtained, how they might set about it, and what the finished presentation should look like. In the early stages of the progression towards autonomy there is nothing wrong in being prescriptive. For many students, the first need is to learn how to deliver the right work at the right time. Of course, no briefing, however skilful will eliminate all the possible questions; but it will succeed in *cutting out the unnecessary*.

Make sure that the students can cope with the resources which have been prescribed for the task

Is the reading level right? Have provisions been made for those who have difficulty in reading? Are there any possible sources of confusion about sequencing within the resources? Are the written assignments (if any) crystal clear? This question of **differentiation** is a major one. Clearly, if students are unable to understand some aspect of the text, activity or task, then interruptions will proliferate. Behaviour also is likely to deteriorate and the teacher's discretionary time will have gone. The third book in the series, *Resources for Flexible Learning,* examines this issue in some depth.

Make sure that the teacher will not be burdened with questions about location of resources or equipment

This may mean delegating some tasks to students. It may also mean investing some time early on in making sure that all students understand where resources are kept and what are the rules for acquiring them.

Encourage the students to seek help from each other before approaching the teacher

This should certainly be encouraged and even demanded. If students are organised in teams, as in the *cabaret* layout, they will already be accustomed to doing this. Whenever a student approaches the teacher with a question it should be assumed that this is only after support from within the team has been sought.

Make explicit arrangements in advance to cope with possible recurring crises

Try to anticipate what these crises are likely to be and make some arrangements so that they are dealt with by the system rather than by *ad hoc* effort on the part of the teacher. An example of these recurring crises might be the students who are fast workers and regularly finish a task before the majority. Why not make available for them a box containing additional tasks of a particularly appealing nature (rewards)?

Analyse the questions that are received from the students with a view to improving the system

Over time this really pays off. For each question consider why it was asked. Was it caused by poor briefing, by inadequate resources, by poor support within the team, or is it just a problem which could easily occur again?

Of course, even if these suggestions are put into practice with enthusiasm they won't entirely eliminate the questions. But that is not the aim. The aim is rather to cut down on the number of questions. And for the most part it will be the trivial, the obvious and the easy that will be eliminated. This then leaves the teacher free to concentrate on some of the heavier problems.

Building on the Strengths

So where does this leave the teacher who has successfully cut out most of the student questions which are simple or trivial or unnecessary? Well, that teacher now enjoys some discretionary time. How might this time be used to best effect? We can now seriously consider setting up meaningful dialogues with our students. Consider these ways in which the teacher might use that discretionary time.

Spend more time listening to individual students

Encourage them to expand on their difficulties and their problems. It not only makes them feel better, but it gives them practice in talking about their work, and it helps the teacher diagnose what the underlying problem might be.

Don't answer a student's question directly

Try to get the student to answer the question, or get another student to join in the discussion. Certainly don't answer the question hurriedly or abruptly.   Gentle prompting, paraphrasing, and redefining the question will all help.

Intervene more

Don't just hang about waiting for their questions. Try a little skilful intervention. Ask some questions of your own. The aim is to find out how well they are understanding and seeing all the implications. Give a little time to fuller explanation or illustration of the ideas.

Form groups

Not permanent groups but little *ad hoc* groups. It is a friendly way of intervening and students enjoy it. They will gain confidence in the small group, and the short experience will add to their motivation.

Don't keep reverting to class teaching

There is always a temptation, whenever a student raises a problem that seems significant, to want to explain it to the whole class. It seems an economical way of doing things. In fact, this is counter-productive. It breaks the concentration of students, and when they are left to pick up the threads of their own work they can feel frustrated. It is nearly always better to tackle the problem with the small groups described above.

Keep a low profile

Do what you want to do quietly and unobtrusively. If you give an impression of bustle and noise, the students will do the same.

D   Conclusion

So the Supervised Study System can represent a good first step for the students who are being trained to accept greater responsibility for their own learning. Coupled with the active learning techniques described in the previous chapter it can add up to a stimulating repertoire.

The system reveals all its potential when the teacher has confidence to allow the students to get on with their work without intervention and when the students are happy and competent to get their problems solved without making excessive demands on the teacher. Most teachers who use this system have experienced this to a greater or lesser degree. The greeting to a visitor to the classroom is often: *Don't worry about the students - they can get on by themselves for a bit.* The build up of responsibility is clearly taking place, and there is potential for progress into new territory. **But everything hinges on the amount of the teacher's discretionary time.**

6

The Independent Learner and the Group Tutorial

THE INDEPENDENT LEARNER AND THE GROUP TUTORIAL

In the last chapter we examined how a teacher might improve the monitoring and support of independent learners. We suggested that in order to do this the teacher had to gain more discretionary time. The only way to do this was to cut out unnecessary and trivial demands that the students might make.

Both teacher and students would gain. The teacher would not be under such pressure and would be able to devote time to students *in more meaningful ways*. There would be more listening, more genuine dialogue, more student participation. The teacher would give greater attention to the briefing of students, to the resources they were using in their tasks, and to the possibilities of support that they could give to each other.

These are substantial benefits in their own right, and a classroom managed in this way would offer stimulating and satisfying experience for the students.

But the most significant thing about this classroom is that there now exists within it a growth point of great potential. We refer to the possibilities for the small group tutorial, led by the teacher. The purpose of this chapter is to explore these exciting possibilities.

A   The Golden Scenario

We have described how a supervised study system can be improved in order to make the interaction between teacher and students much more meaningful. By devoting just a little more time to each encounter the teacher is able to learn more about the student, get the student to contribute more, and to raise the level of the student's thinking and commitment.

This kind of high quality support works particularly well when small *ad hoc* groups are formed for a few minutes. It gives a sense of collaborative working. Students prompt and help each other, or even vie with each other; they are spared the psychological pressure of being the sole focus of the teacher's attention; they share a sense of achievement and often make commitments to go on sharing or supporting. When the encounter is finished the students disperse and resume their individual or paired work. The experience has been an enjoyable interlude within the normal routine.

There is also the benefit that the teacher's time is being used economically. Instead of working a path stolidly through 30 individual students, the teacher may accomplish just as much by 4 or 5 encounters with small *ad hoc* groups.

Do the students lose the personal touch through being grouped in this way? It may happen sometimes, but the more likely outcome is that the students get a strong feeling of belonging which is very powerful.

This is the *golden scenario*. It is the starting position from which most good systems of independent learning grow.

It would be a mistake however to rush on. There is a lot to be said for spending time improving and refining the *supervised study system*. Students need to be trained to work effectively in this way. Here are some suggestions for improvement and consolidation, which should help provide a firm base for the next advance.

- Frequently discuss the system with the students. They need to understand what your objectives are.

- Praise all examples of enterprise and responsibility.

- Take every opportunity to teach them about their own thought processes. So you need to add to their vocabulary: - **analysis, conjecture, hypothesis, evidence,** and so on. Praise the thoughtful response, especially one that is (usefully) wrong.

- Constantly emphasise their independence. Praise the student who perseveres and tries to get solutions.

- Monitor carefully your own use of time. Have you succeeded in increasing the amount of your discretionary time? Try to increase it without abandoning your reasonable level of support for the students.

B   The Group Tutorial

Where students are working well under the supervised study system described in the last chapter, the teacher may feel that they are capable of advancing still further down the road towards autonomy. The way ahead is through the group tutorial. Consider this assertion and this problem.

The Assertion   **The small group tutorial holds out more promise of raising educational standards than any other single strategy.** Within the small group the teacher can offer support and guidance which is tailor-made, and can raise the intellectual level of the experience quite dramatically. Within the small group each individual student feels a stronger sense of personal worth and responsibility.

The Problem **How can we run these small-group tutorials when class sizes are so large and syllabus pressures so demanding?**

The assertion is a bold one, but more and more teachers would now support it. And a substantial number are proving that the problem can be overcome. If this is true we are living in exciting times.

In order to do justice to this important subject **Book 4** within this series is devoted to the subject of *Tutoring (see page 124 for details). But it is necessary here, from the point of view of classroom management, to provide a glimpse of the vision, and to take a detailed look at ways of realising it.*

C The Vision of a Group Tutorial

For the moment let us pretend that the problem (the class size and the pressure of syllabus) doesn't exist. Let us try to describe how we would like to organise the learning of a small group of students using all the advantages of the small numbers and applying our best thinking about the skills of teaching and learning. This should give us a *vision* of our ultimate goal. We know that, in practice, we are not likely to realise the vision quickly and we shall never realise it entirely, but at least we shall have something to aim for. As soon as we have described the vision we shall start looking at ways of making progress towards it.

An Overview of the Group Tutorial

The group tutorial is an opportunity to provide an intensive educational experience. It penetrates deeply into educational objectives. In the small group the teacher can tune in accurately to the existing knowledge and readiness of the students and help them to raise the intellectual level. In the small group the teacher can demonstrate the personal worth of each individual and encourage each one to contribute. In the small group the students can support each other and use each other as resources in natural, conversational ways.

The atmosphere of the small group can so easily become calm and positive and friendly, yet disciplined and purposeful. Students get a

sense of their own worth and are eager to take on responsibility. The
occasion has a feeling of privacy, and students are not afraid to confess
to ignorance or confusion, and not afraid to ask for help. Throughout
the teacher is able to become a good role model of the mature learner -
intellectually honest, **respectful** of the contributions of others,
disciplined in the pursuit of agreed objectives, and **rigorous** in
evaluation. And there are the countless opportunities to teach them
about the skills that they need - the skills of working as a member of a
group; the skills of finding out and studying; the skills of reporting and
presenting.

The Structure and Processes of the Group Tutorial

The Size of the Group

An optimum size is probably about 5, although successful tutorials can
be conducted with any group in the range 4 to 8. Outside this range the
problems increase rapidly. As the group gets smaller the variety of
contribution is diminished and the tutorial may begin to lack vitality. As
the group gets bigger it becomes increasingly difficult to keep all
students equally involved, and to allow sufficient time to each
individual.

There is also a limitation on the number of tutorial groups that one
teacher can successfully manage within a single class. It is wise to keep
the number below 6. So for a class of 30 students it might be best to
organise in 5 tutorial groups of 6 students in each.

The Composition of the Group

A good mixture of abilities and personalities often makes the most
interesting tutorial group. So normally a group would include both boys
and girls, and should cover a fairly wide band of ability in the subject.
It is not wise to attempt to organise tutorial groups by strict ability
streaming; the weakest group presents too many problems. On the other
hand many teachers find that small groups which span the whole range
of ability are difficult to manage. Some experimentation is worth while,
bearing in mind the subject matter and the characteristics of the students
themselves. There is certainly no universal solution to this problem.

The Life-span of the Tutorial Group

We should certainly aim to get the benefits of some continuity. So the
group should have a reasonable life-span. But there are good arguments
for not making the arrangement permanent. An occasional change
during a year gives the students an opportunity to establish new

relationships and have a sense of a fresh start. It also gives the teacher the opportunity to reorganise in order to fit the needs of a new component in a programme of study.

The Frequency and Length of Tutorials

The choice is clearly between longer tutorials held only occasionally, and shorter tutorials held very frequently. The former arrangement tends to suit the more mature and experienced students; the latter the younger and less experienced. The range of possibilities is very wide. At one extreme a good sixth form group might pursue a topic through independent study with a weekly tutorial lasting an hour. At the other extreme a teacher working with a large lower school class may feel that each group should have perhaps two or three very short tutorials during an hour long period; the size of the tasks set would be also very small.

The Agenda of the Tutorial

Tutorials can have many different aims. So it follows that they must have different agendas. No two tutorials are likely to be the same. It all depends on the needs of the learning situation. Here is a list of possible agendas:

(a) A briefing tutorial.   This is required at the beginning of a new topic or at a significant point in the development of the topic. The purpose is to make sure that the students have thought through all the implications of the work that they are going to do independently. They will need help in the following:

- clarifying the objectives of the work
- exploring the resources that are available, making some judgements about the contribution that each resource might make, looking at the strengths and weaknesses of each item which will be used
- devising a strategy for tackling the work - the sequence of activities, the relative importance to be attached to different components, the difficulties and problems which might be encountered, the opportunities for extending the work if time allows
- agreeing the nature of the finished product - in what form will it appear, how big will it be, when exactly is it due?

The briefing tutorial is probably the most common type of tutorial and probably the most important. Setting students complex independent learning assignments without proper briefing is the surest recipe for failure.

(b) The Review Tutorial. This agenda is also frequently used. The students have completed a learning assignment and the purpose of the tutorial is to review and assess their work. Some of the possible components are set out below.

- The student's own report on the work - what has been done, what has not been done, what has proved difficult, what has proved particularly interesting, what implications are there for the work as a whole.

- A comparison of the approach adopted by different students with reflection on the significance of the differences.

- An assessment of each student's work (it being assumed that the teacher has had the opportunity to look at the work before the tutorial), done publicly with the active involvement of all the group.

- The recording of achievement and targets for future work on a record or profile sheet. This will usually be a formative document, but if the tutorial is at the end of a piece of coursework or module then the records might be summative.

(c) The Discussion Tutorial. This is required where a topic requires the students to reflect and consider different interpretations of facts. A well-structured discussion enables students to try out the ideas and engage in critical debate about them.

(d) A Coaching Tutorial. This is an occasion where the teacher reverts to teaching in a more traditional sense. It is needed where there are particularly difficult concepts and ideas to be mastered. The small group provides the best environment for the analysis of the ideas and diagnosis of problems. The weak student gets the best possible support here because of the feedback which the skilful teacher is constantly seeking.

(e) A Planning Tutorial. This is similar to the briefing tutorial except that the purpose may be to look further ahead and to take a wider view than the next piece of work. This is the sort of tutorial which might be conducted when students are about to embark on major coursework projects. In such circumstances many teachers are now using study guides as part of the agenda. This topic is explored in more depth in both **Book 3** and **Book 4** of the series. (See pages123 &124 for details.)

(f) A Managerial Tutorial . Sometimes the group may need a simple business meeting to get a lot of arrangements sorted out. This is a valuable experience especially when it is conducted in a business-like and disciplined way.

(g) Mixed Agendas.   Often a tutorial has a specific purpose and the agenda is designed accordingly. But there are also more general tutorials. In these the characteristics of more than one of the main types described above are combined. For example, a tutorial may start with a review of work completed and then go on to plan the next piece of work. Or a tutorial may carry out a small piece of planning and then spend the rest of the time on discussion of some of the more important issues.

But whatever the needs the agenda of the tutorial must be explicit. Students must know what the purposes are, and they must be encouraged to learn to work to an agenda.

Educational Objectives

The tutorial can also be described in terms of educational objectives - in other words asking the question, *what differences are we trying to bring about in our students?* There are four categories to be considered.

(a) The intellectual.   We are trying to encourage them to use their thinking skills and not merely learn things by rote. The skilful tutor is constantly finding ways of getting students to express themselves clearly and to become more aware of their own thought processes. It is all about structuring, analysing, evaluating, and the use of high-level vocabulary.

(b) The personal.   Within the small group the individual counts for more. The good tutorial demonstrates concern for the well-being of the individual and for personal development, over and above the immediate needs of the task in hand. The atmosphere is warm and supportive, and this builds feelings of self-respect and respect for others. Learning takes on a new *personal* meaning.

(c) The social.   Within the small group the relationship between the members is a powerful contributor to success. Students learn to cooperate, to use each other as sounding boards and as sources of knowledge and inspiration. They learn to compete and challenge and argue a case, but without losing their mutual respect (or their tempers!).

(d) The managerial.   The tutorial group is also a disciplined task-oriented group. There is frequent reference to objectives and standards and deadlines. A crisp business-like style helps to make sure that the group has a constant feeling of progress and achievement.

Of course this is ambitious. High achievement in these four areas demands skill, particularly in balancing the four main areas. Sometimes the different objectives seem mutually exclusive. It is easy to recognise, for example, that a tutorial may become so task-oriented that it partly inhibits the development of the personal objectives.

But the important point is that the tutorial is small enough to enable the teacher to adjust in sensitive ways. And this is one of the aspects of tutoring which is so intriguing.

Styles and Techniques

The styles and techniques used in a tutorial reflect closely the educational objectives. The style is best summarised by a quotation.

Achieving Flexibility by Empowering People:

1.   Involve everyone in everything.

2.   Use self-managing teams.

3.   Listen, celebrate, recognise.

(Tom Peters. Thriving on Chaos. Pan. London. 1988)

The detail of the techniques is a big subject in its own right and is dealt with in the separate handbook in this series. But the quotation above provides pointers in the right direction. The teacher who is new to tutoring could not do better than to use this short quotation as a personal check-list for self-evaluation.

D   Towards the Group Tutorial

Most teachers would find themselves in sympathy with the vision of the group tutorial which has just been described. They will also experience a sense of frustration that the conditions under which they work do not seem to encourage progress in that direction.

Progress seems to be easiest in the sixth forms where numbers are often small, the students are more mature and sometimes highly intelligent, and there is a tradition of private unsupervised study. The problem is at its worst in the large classes of the lower school where the students are younger, of mixed ability, and there is a need for them to be supervised at all times. We shall concentrate our thinking at the lower school end!

How can we extend the small group tutorial within the confines of the lower school classroom? The answer is with difficulty and slowly! Yet it is amazing what can be achieved. The following suggestions should help.

Improve the golden scenario

Our golden scenario was the improved *supervised study system*. The key was that the teacher had gained more discretionary time so that encounters with students could become more meaningful and less hasty and abrupt. It is worth working at this over a period of time. The simple indicator of success is to measure the intervals of time between requests for help initiated by the students. When five minutes can go by with the students all busy on task, the teacher can begin to feel that real progress is being made. It is partly a question of encouraging the students to be independent and to support each other, and partly of making sure that briefing, resources, and housekeeping have all been attended to. The last chapter explained these ideas in more detail.

It is only when the supervised study system is working really well that the class is ready to make the move towards the tutorial system.

Seize opportunities to work with groups rather than individuals

Whenever it makes sense to do so, respond to an individual's question by involving a group of students. You might already have the class working in active learning teams and it would make sense to use such a ready-made group. But it is easy to involve a small number of students. Make it into a little *ad hoc* tutorial. Get the members to try to answer the question. Point out some of the interesting implications. Take the opportunity to check their understanding of the task and the subject matter. And leave it at that! It should only take a minute or two, and you can then get back to overall supervision of the whole class. But the students are beginning to learn to operate as a team.

Team build

We have already discussed the importance and the possibilities of team building in a previous chapter. It needs doing for the tutorial groups from the very beginning. The more they are proud of their membership and have a feeling of solidarity with each other, the more effective the tutorials can be.

Make plans for the transition between whole class work and work which is driven by tutorial

It simply is not possible to leap from whole class teaching into tutorial led work in one move. What is the rest of the class doing while you are briefing the first tutorial group? And the second tutorial group?

The transition has to be made through the supervised study system. Set all the students a common task by whole class briefing. When you are satisfied that it is going well and you have sufficient discretionary time then start giving each tutorial group in turn a short briefing for a short task.

Use mini-tutorials

In the early stages, when students are still relatively inexperienced, these tasks and briefing sessions should be very short indeed. We want to try to get the system rolling without risking major disaster. These mini - tutorials are an excellent way of getting the students accustomed to the cycle and aware of the fact that the review of their work will be thorough.

Quite clearly there are some big compromises here. You are not likely to achieve the vision of a group tutorial that we have painted in this chapter. But it is a progressive training towards independence, and mini-tutorials conducted in this way mark an important step in the right direction.

Leave time to reflect and evaluate

It would be wise to leave a little time for reflection and evaluation. So after a few lessons experimenting with the mini-tutorial it would be useful to consider the strengths and weaknesses of what has been achieved so far. Improvements for the next round could be considered. It is always worth while to seek the opinions and advice of the students themselves. If they feel part of an interesting development they will not only be helpful in thinking through the issues, but will also work better in class (at least, in the short term which will be a bonus during the early stages!).

E   The Group Tutorial and Independent Learning

An Important Relationship

In our overview of classroom management we listed some of the common forms of independent learning activities. The relationship between these activities and the group tutorial needs to be carefully considered.

The diagram below looks deceptively simple.

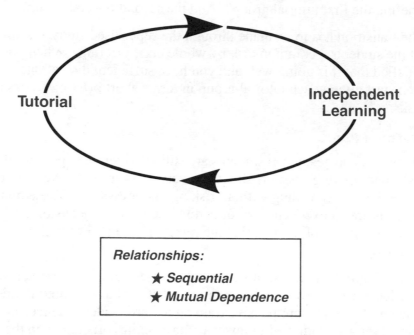

The arrows might at first seem to be just showing a sequence of activities: a tutorial is followed by a period of independent learning, which is in turn followed by a tutorial, and so on. This is perfectly true. But the arrows also demonstrate mutual dependence. The independent learning *depends on* a high quality tutorial. But also the existence of a tutorial *depends on* the students being able to work independently. The two are inextricably linked. And for the teacher who is trying to get independent learning established this is a typical 'chicken and egg' situation. One cannot make progress on one side without there being equivalent progress on the other.

So the good tutorial is helping students to plan and prepare effectively for their independent work, but is also providing a forum for their reporting and reflecting. It has a business-like aim, but it also is an opportunity for discussion and a meeting of minds. We can illustrate this in practice by reference to a common type of independent learning.

Project Work : An Illustration

Project work is increasingly required or offered as part of the course for external examinations. The aim is to broaden students'educational experience and to give them opportunities for independent work.

Although a student may choose a personal topic and will be assessed individually, there is still a strong case for the tutorial support to be arranged in small groups. This is much better than forcing the student into isolation for this work. The student can gain experience and intellectual stimulation from membership of a group, and the simple sharing of ideas and approaches can be valuable.

The First Briefing

The purpose of the first tutorial must be to carry out the initial planning. The student should be asked to come prepared with details of his/her interpretation of what has to be done,and in turn should speak about:

- the objectives of the project[1]
- the limits of the project (what should be included or left out)
- the resources likely to be required
- what the end-product will be (to be described in detail)
- a proposed calendar of activities
- any perceived problems.

There should be brief discussion by all the members of each project and the student should be encouraged to make notes as to what has to be done immediately in order to get the work plan into a satisfactory shape.

Subsequent tutorials

These could be used in a variety of ways. Here are three possibilities:

☐ The group works as a whole, listening to interim reports given by individual members - asking questions, making suggestions, and offering opinions about what has been done so far.

☐ The group works as a whole, discussing strategies and tactics for the learning tasks that are being undertaken. This is an opportunity for sharing ideas and information about resources.

☐ The members of the group work on their own tasks, but the tutor withdraws individuals for intensive tutorial support.

Whatever the style used the students must learn to make notes during the tutorial and to regard their notes as a form of contract between them

1   *Study Guides* provide the perfect agenda for such tutorials - see page 125 and Book 3

and the tutor. Many teachers have designed their own contract forms to help students use a structured approach.

Between Tutorials

Students are likely to require help between tutorials. But the teacher should aim to cut this to a minimum:

* concentrate on high quality briefing at the tutorial
* encourage students to plan their contribution to the tutorial so that they cover all the points there and then.

Of course, this is a counsel of perfection. But it is worth some effort to try to stop project work becoming an excessive burden for all.

F   The Tutorial in its Own Right

The tutorial is an educational experience in its own right

It is important to say this because it has sometimes been assumed that the tutorial is purely a support arrangement for independent work. This implies that it is only when working independently that the student's responsibility is being developed.

It is important to express the opposite view. Consider our own responsibilities as members of a profession. Does our responsibility manifest itself when we are allowed the privilege of working quietly on our own? Or is it more apparent when we have to work with other people - planning, justifying, negotiating, explaining, requesting, reporting, questioning? These are surely the real indicators of responsibility. And it is in the small group tutorial that the student begins to learn these skills of adult life.

The teacher's role is crucial

Working as a member of a small group is a sophisticated adult activity. Our students need their teacher in this situation more than they need anything else. **It is the teacher who sets the standards and the style and provides the role model.** This in no way contradicts the student-centred philosophy that guides the system.

So it is vital that the students should experience the well-conducted teacher-led tutorial before being asked to embark on group activities in which they are entirely self-managing. This latter is the ultimate objective, but we are taking a step by step approach. Our next chapter considers these possibilities.

7

The Self Managing Team

THE SELF-MANAGING TEAM

This chapter takes our learners a further step forward on the road towards autonomy. It explores the possibilities of much greater freedom and discretion for the learner.

The idea of the self-managing team is an attractive one and it is highly regarded in the adult world as a better way of getting people to give their best and to get a high level of satisfaction from their work.

The basic principle of the self-managing team is that the team decides how best to tackle a job, and allocates responsibilities and tasks to the individual member. So individual work is not at all excluded.

The question for teachers is whether this way of working can be used with young students in school. The answer depends of course, on their state of readiness. If they have grown accustomed to taking on greater responsibility through active assignments and group tutorials, then it is likely that they could begin to make progress on the lines suggested in this chapter. However, as in all classroom management, it is wise to proceed with caution and not to build up expectations too rapidly.

Certainly all students should have had some experience of the self-managing team by the time they reach the age of 16. **It seems reasonable to suppose that it should be part of the regular experience of students in the 16 - 19 age range.**

A
The Case for the Self-Managing Team

The case for the self-managing team rests mainly on its potential for increasing the motivation of its members.

These are the features of the self-managing team which improve motivation:

- the members of the team make their own decisions as to how the work is to be tackled
- the teacher provides an information and ideas service which is designed to help teams develop their own thinking
- the teacher offers support to the team which generates self-confidence and ambition without undermining its autonomy
- the teacher acts as a sounding board for the team's ideas and plans
- the teacher acts as a coach, training members in the roles, responsibilities and techniques of the self-managing team.

When these features are present the team members begin to get a sense of ownership about the work and a strong desire to succeed. They begin to support each other and to seek assistance from each other. They begin to know the deep satisfaction which comes from working as a member of an effective and respected group. They look upon the teacher as a consultant. **It is in this sort of atmosphere that knowledge and understanding grow.**

Of course, a word of caution is necessary. The features of the self-managing team described above cannot be put into place instantly. They are the result of a progressive training towards autonomy, and almost invariably are a development from some of the systems and techniques which have been described in previous chapters.

It is not possible to generalise as to when students are ready for the self-managing team. Some 11 year olds will work well in self-managing teams; some 17 year olds may be completely disorientated. The technique is to introduce the idea slowly and on a small scale. This gives the teacher an opportunity to identify needs and respond to them; and it gives the students time to adjust to the new demands that are being made on them.

Coaching in the roles, responsibilities and techniques should have started during teacher-led tutorials.

B   The Purposes and Functions of the Self-Managing Team

The underlying purpose is to increase the opportunities for student-student interaction. When they are accustomed to talk to each other about their work, in the absence of the teacher, the prospects for their learning are very good indeed. Each individual student begins at his/her own starting point. Within any team there are bound to be differences in knowledge, experience, and attitudes.

But each individual student will influence the direction in which the team's thinking develops - setting the pace, asking the questions, formulating the answers, and criticising the general direction of the argument. It is through this process that the student is helped to assume a responsibility for the learning, and to develop a sense of ownership of new knowledge and understanding. The knowledge has become *personal* knowledge, through the *participation* and *commitment* of the learner.

But it is inevitably a slow process. The students may not always reach the conclusions and vocabulary that the teacher would like to see. The temptation is to intervene too frequently, *to get them on the right track*. But this would be an unfortunate judgement. The students need time to express themselves in their own way, to explore ideas, to use their imagination, to share in the formulation of ideas and solutions to problems, and to plan and organise the work of the group. This is not to imply that the teacher should totally abdicate during periods of team activity. Preparation, follow-up, and timely intervention are all vital. It all depends on some very fine judgements on the part of the teacher.

C Criteria for the Formation of Self-Managing Teams

Group size and composition

These questions have already been discussed in the chapters on teams in active learning and teacher-led tutorials. Similar principles should apply here. In fact, it is very likely that it will be the same group that will operate in different modes according to different needs:

- as a team within an active class teaching lesson
- as a tutorial group for supporting independent learning
- as an occasional self-managing team.

But we have also made the point that these teams should not be regarded as permanent. There is a lot to commend the idea of using a team for a particular job in a programme of study, with the assumption that it will be disbanded when the job has been done. This arrangement gives students a wider experience and helps sharpen the focus on specific objectives and the need to be business-like.

Leadership

If the teacher is not going to lead the group the question of leadership needs to be addressed. In many adult groups of five or six participants the group can often be leaderless because the members are sufficiently sophisticated to be able to handle skilfully any tendency to dominate or disrupt. This is a lot to ask of young students. So it is better to think of a nominated leader. This decision could be made by the teacher, but it is better to encourage the group to choose its own leader for a particular purpose. This means that the role would be a temporary one and leadership would therefore come from different members at different times and for different purposes. It would help if, when a new task is being considered, the teacher invited each team to choose a new leader. In this way most of the group members would get a chance, if they so wished.

The teacher's coaching of the self-managing team could usefully concentrate on the guidance and support of the leader. Quite young students can learn how to apply simple rules of procedure, how to move the discussion along by asking stimulating and exploratory questions, how to keep reminding the team of its goals, how to summarise in order to help everyone's understanding.

However there may well be groups and situations where the teacher feels that the team can operate without a nominated leader. This is stimulating and well worth trying, particularly in the 16 to 19 age range.

Individual Responsibilities

In addition to the elected leader it may be useful to encourage teams to give specific jobs to the individual members. The team could agree a short job description for each job (helped by a model which the teacher has provided). The jobs can be rotated. Typical jobs might be *timekeeper, secretary, process observer, resources manager.* Ideally everyone in the team should have a job.

D   Occasions for Self-Managing Teams

Where do the self-managing teams meet?

In an ideal world each team would have its own home-base. Conditions are unlikely to permit this, and many teachers might be cautious about such an arrangement. But the alternative of keeping all the groups inside the same classroom does present difficulties of space and disturbance.

Compromises are worth investigating. For example, an adjacent store room or even the corridor outside might offer space for one group which would relieve the pressure. At all times the teacher is trying to push forward the frontiers of independence. An important principle is to give a group more responsibility *just before* the members seem ready for it.

When do the best opportunities occur for self-managing teams?

Logically this kind of group work should come at a fairly late stage in the study of a particular topic. In the early stages the students will have had the need for general orientation and stimulus and motivation, and this can be best provided by the teacher. Then there is a stage at which more information is accumulated, ideas developed, observations and experiences enlarged, and this can often be done by individual working. Group work comes most appropriately when the individual members of the group are *ready*. This state of readiness is reached when one or more of the following has happened:

- students have spent some time working on their own, finding out information, developing ideas or practising skills

- students have received a common stimulus during which there has been no opportunity for them to react, other than privately, eg, viewing live television or listening to live radio

- students have shared a common experience where there has been much opportunity for individual observation and personal reflection, eg, an educational visit

- students are known to have had some personal experiences in their out-of school lives which will have some bearing on the work.

The message is that there can be no worthwhile group work until the individual members can bring to the group their individual and different knowledge, observations, experiences, perceptions, and attitudes. And they must have had time to acquire all this.

What are the typical occasions?

These are very similar to the occasions when the team is set small assignments in the whole class active learning system. The important difference is in the scale of the assignment and its duration. In the self-managing team there is a much bigger assumption made about the organising capabilities of the team.

Some of the suggestions made here could form the nucleus of a personal checklist. Eventually the repertoire available to a subject department could be very large, and individual teachers would benefit by knowing which colleagues had already had some experience of a particular technique.

Experts

Challenge each group to become as expert as they can on one particular aspect of a topic. The topic would probably have to be negotiated so that unnecessary overlapping was prevented. Give them plenty of time to prepare and lots of advice and help with resources and general organisation. Then each group in turn becomes an expert panel, either making a presentation to the whole class, or responding to questions.

Mastery Learning

For the topic being studied define as accurately as you can the standard expected of every student. Give the teams a good idea of the kind of test which will be used. Challenge each team to bring all its members up to standard within a limited time. Encourage mutual aid.

Pass the Problem

Invite each team to prepare a problem for consideration by another team. Advise them that the problem must be a big one which will require an extended answer. They must avoid simple questions of fact. So they will probably include questions starting with *Why...?* or *How....?* When the problems have been prepared they are passed on to another team. Each team is then given time to work on the problem it has been given before being asked to make a statement giving its considered response.

Twenty Questions

This is a much shorter exercise but it can be effective if teams are allowed time to work out their strategies. First, each team chooses an animal, vegetable or mineral from the topic being studied. Another team is then allowed 20 questions to discover what the object is, but only through questions that can be answered by YES or NO. Encourage debate within the questioning group to try to determine the best strategy.

Delegated Tasks

Invite the team to approach a topic or project by delegating work to its individual members. Each team member is allocated part of the topic and at the end of an agreed time is expected to: (a) provide a set of notes to summarise the main points, (b) present questions or problems for the team to discuss, and (c) provide test questions for the individual team members.

Games and Simulations

Where these are available the self-managing team is the ideal way of using them. At their best they can contribute a great deal to the educational development of the students taking part. There are likely to be gains in communication skills, in general motivation, in knowledge acquisition, in creativity, and in inter-personal skills. The demands on the students are considerable and advice and support are crucial.

Structured Discussion

Invite the team to explore a whole topic through discussion. Start them off with an agenda but leave plenty of space for their own directions. Give them lots of help in matters of timing and procedures.

Techniques and Processes for Self-Managing Teams

The typical occasions described above represent a formidable challenge to any group of young students. Even if they have been well grounded in more active ways of learning and have had experience of well-conducted tutorials they will still not find life easy in the self-managing team. So they need some high quality advice and support.

There may be a temptation to put them through an intensive training in the techniques and processes *before* asking them to work as members of a team. Undoubtedly something can be achieved in this way, but these skills, like most skills, are best acquired on the job. So the teacher needs to have a repertoire of advice and training *up the sleeve* ready to be used whenever the students seem to be ready and in need of it.

So the suggestions made here should not be delivered to the students as a course. Instead they should be used as brief interludes during the work, giving the students the opportunity to reflect on the processes which are at work and how they might make more effective use of their own and their fellow students' talents.

House Rules

Some simple house rules will be useful. They need to be specially designed for each class, bearing in mind age, experience, special subject requirements, and competence in self-management. The following suggestions give an indication of the kind of rules that may be helpful.

- On each occasion the leader will decide, after consultation with the team members, exactly what the agenda is to be, and the scribe will write it down where everyone can see it.

- Members of the team speak only when invited to do so by the leader.

- The leader has a responsibility to make sure that the discussion and the action is fairly shared among the team members.

- At the end of each session the scribe will write down what has been agreed and check that everyone has accepted it. If action by team members is called for then it needs to be recorded *what* is to be done, by *whom* and *when* by.

After having received a basic framework of rules members of the team should be invited formally to adopt them and then occasionally to add rules of their own in order to make their collaboration even more effective.

Thinking Skills

Teams need help in setting about their tasks in an intelligent manner. It is wrong to assume that they can operate in a sophisticated way without some training. Young students can learn better thinking strategies. The best way is to give them some simple models to use. These will serve as props to help them set about their deliberations in a structured manner. When they find these successful they will be eager to build on them.

Show them how to look at a question systematically

Ready-made mini-agendas have proved very helpful. For example:

Strengths

Weaknesses

Opportunities

Threats

When faced with an issue to be discussed the team may use the **SWOT** technique as a ready made mini-agenda. All members will first concentrate on the strengths of the argument or arrangement; then they will examine its weaknesses, and so on.

The technique helps to make sure that the students look at every side of a question and do not leap into instant conclusions based on the first most persuasive argument they hear.

Here are some more examples of mini-agendas.

The **ADD** technique:

Advantages

Disadvantages

Discussion points

Factors

> Factors affecting **oneself**
>
> Factors affecting **other people**
>
> Factors affecting **society**
>
> Factors to be **ignored**.

Time Scales

> **Long** term
>
> **Medium** term
>
> **Short** term.

Teams should be encouraged to develop their own mini-agendas as procedures for tackling problems.

Train them to see a problem from the opposite point of view

This should not be done casually or lightly. Encourage them to develop the opposite view in a full-blooded way, using some of the mini-agendas. In this way they will learn to get a much better understanding of the strengths and weaknesses of an argument.

Train them in the development of alternative solutions

The principles are the same. Rather than leaping into advocacy of an attractive solution, they should spend time working out the detail of the alternatives, even if, at the end, they will come to reject them. They need to have it explained to them that original thinking often starts by trying to justify what seems unjustifiable.

Group Skills

The members of a team also need help in recognising the processes which are at work within the group.

- What proportion of the talk does each member have?
- What roles are the various members playing? *Initiator? Leader? Coordinator? Agitator? Scapegoat? Builder?*
- What kinds of contributions to the discussion are being made?

  > **Questions**, asking for information, help, opinion?
  >
  > **Answers**, offering suggestions, opinion, information?
  >
  > **Comments** that are supportive, friendly and understanding?
  >
  > **Remarks** that are hostile, tense and disagreeing?

If the team has appointed a *process consultant* that student should be invited periodically to report on the effectiveness of the group as a unit. Discussion should follow and the leader should aim to get clear understanding and commitment so that the team can operate more effectively in the future.

The skills of working with people are a subject in their own right. It is worth finding out what is happening in the school generally to encourage students to think on these lines. Often there is valuable work going on within a tutorial or Personal and Social Education Programme which should be transferred into the other subjects of the curriculum.

8

Inter-Personal Relations

INTER-PERSONAL RELATIONS

Expanding the repertoire of teaching and learning seems fine, but teachers are often anxious that the greater complexity of classroom life may lead to bigger problems in maintaining a smooth working atmosphere. The classroom could so easily become a haven for laziness and disinclination and a hiding place for disruption and malice.

The truth of the matter is probably that the broad repertoire classroom has a much greater range of possibilities. With careless handling the worst could happen and standards of behaviour and attitude would deteriorate. On the other hand, the student-centred approaches do improve motivation, and when working in small groups or as individuals, students do develop different relationships with their fellows and with their teacher.

So we ought to lean towards optimism. If we can manage the inter-personal relations with skill we can achieve a much more positive atmosphere leading to more effective learning. So this must be given high priority. It is an ever present need. Most teachers acquire their skills in this aspect of management through experience and intuition. However it is hoped that the analysis in this chapter will help to heighten awareness and reinforce some of the best techniques.

A   The Background

There has always been a steady flow of publicity which claims that standards of discipline in schools have declined. There is no shortage of *evidence*: aggressive and disruptive behaviour, acts of violence against persons and property, use of alcohol, drug abuse, defiance of authority.

It is true that many teachers have to spend a disproportionate amount of their time dealing with disruptive students and the consequences of their actions. They could also add to the list of *evidence* many other manifestations which do not make the headlines, but which do make the teacher's work much more difficult: boredom, unwillingness to cooperate, anxiety, indifferent health, and other symptoms of underlying distress.

There are some who, in the face of all these problems, have abandoned educational objectives in favour of counselling and crisis management. They argue that it is impossible to teach these students anything until their personal lives have been sorted out. The trouble is that this is never achieved. There are others who declare themselves to be *teachers, not social workers*, hoping that the problems will go away, or that somebody else will deal with them. There is a third group, and they are probably the majority, who are desperately torn between the two points of view outlined above. They appreciate that students do not live their lives in compartments, and that success can only occur across a wide front embracing every aspect of a student's life and development. The solutions are not easy.

This is not the place to attempt a detailed analysis of the causes of the problems. However a summary of factors is given below without any attempt to elaborate.

Society as a whole

- The economic problems of the country reduce the individual's feeling of personal financial security.
- Today's organisations are bigger, and seem to offer less scope for individuality.
- International tensions and the threat of global war frequently reassert themselves.
- There has been increased use of violence by small groups in order to attain political or personal gain.
- The decay of inner city areas has proceed faster than the measures to combat it.
- Unfair discrimination is still a feature of our society.

The Home

- Physical neglect - meals, clothing, health.
- Mental neglect - absence of conversation *(language deprivation)*, a contempt for anything intellectual, the determined exclusion of rationality as a basis of decision making.
- Emotional neglect - depravity in the home, emotional cruelty, mental abnormality in the home, a lack of love.

The School

- The impersonal and insensitive regime.
- The focus that is exclusively on academic achievement.
- The use of excessive regulation creating an impression of distrust.
- A lack of respect for the opinions or feelings of students.

Adolescence

- Tensions resulting from physical changes.
- The drive towards independence which is not always consistent and smooth.
- The youth sub-culture and the power of peer pressure.

With all this to contend with it seems a miracle that so many of our adolescents are good students with a strong sense of their responsibilities and opportunities. We need to do everything in our power to help them.

Success in building good personal relations within the classroom depends on both **long-term strategies** and **short-term tactics.**

B   Classroom Strategies

What is it that marks out the successful and respected teacher whose students seem naturally to work with positive and constructive attitudes? What advice might such a teacher give to a beginner?

Get the 'knowledge'

Like the London taxi driver who needs to know the detail of the city, the teacher needs to develop a deep understanding of the environment of the students. This means knowing about the catchment area of the school, knowing about students and their families, knowing about students' outside interests, knowing about students' other activities within the school, knowing about the school - its traditions, its rules and its events. Encyclopaedic knowledge of this kind is vital. It is what distinguishes the established teacher from the newcomer (however senior). A wise teacher builds that knowledge continually.

Prepare thoroughly

Prepare teaching thoroughly - materials, activities, assessments. When a student knows that the teacher is filling time, or having to change activities because materials cannot be found, or is not prepared for problems which emerge, then respect and confidence ebb away.

Prepare administrative matters thoroughly. Keep on top of routine. Nothing undermines a student's confidence more than a teacher who is flustered.

Build an image

Students tune in to the image which the teacher presents to them from the very first appearance. Subconsciously they are watching and recording every initiative, every reaction, every expression of feeling. It all builds up into an image.

The **knowledge** already discussed is an important aspect of the image. Students must feel that the teacher knows about them, their families, and their home area. They must also get the impression that the teacher knows the school systems and procedures thoroughly. For a newcomer it is worth while deliberately setting out to demonstrate early **mastery** in order to make the point to the students. A little name-dropping or a little demonstration of inside information can often help!

Then create a serious impression of purpose. Trying to seek quick and easy popularity through ingratiating practices or being *with it* can be counter-productive. The old cynical advice: *Don't smile until Christmas* has some force. Students come to like their teachers first by **respecting** them and then happily discovering that they are also very human. The serious and firm impression of purpose is conveyed by being thorough in one's own contributions and in the demands made on the students. This means attention to detail, and an assumption that students will take their work seriously and with a sense of responsibility.

There needs also to be an impression of **strength** and **resolution.** While the normal stance will be calm and pleasant, the students should soon discover how the teacher will react in a crisis. The newcomer needs to demonstrate fairly early that he/she will not flinch from responsibilities and will be contemptuous of any attempt to start *negotiations* after there has been a flagrant breach of rules or instructions.

But this needs to be balanced by an impression of a **caring adult**. Every opportunity should be taken, and it is often outside the classroom, of establishing some personal contact with as many individual students as possible. The discovery of a shared interest, a word of praise after an achievement, a word of sympathy after a disappointment, a little practical help or advice, an appreciative word to a parent (who is sure to pass it on), can all help to establish a bond. Most teachers can recall instances of much improved relationships after they have taken part in some informal activity such as camping, expeditions, social work, and sporting activities.

C Classroom Tactics

Long-term strategies can help a teacher build up good standards of personal relationships which result in good discipline. Nevertheless, teachers are dealing with young people who may not be capable of coping with all the stresses of their lives and who often react by laziness, insubordination, defiance, mischief, aggression, or destructiveness. It is a pity when these behaviours are allowed to undermine the building up of good classroom practice which is designed to help students learn effectively and take on greater responsibility.

We need to examine now the tactics of the classroom which will help to avoid or prevent these troubles, or if they do occur, to handle them in the most effective way.

Unfortunately, advice about tactics is less reliable than advice about general strategies. The complexity of classroom life is responsible for this. Classroom life is multidimensional, with many different kinds of activities, many different purposes, and many people having different needs and different styles. Things happen simultaneously. There is an air of immediacy about the place. At any one time the teacher is considering what to do next, thinking ahead about the development of the lesson, watching the progress of students, looking out for anything which might disrupt the smooth flow of the work. And then there are the unpredictables, such as the interruption from outside, the unforeseen difficulties, and the minor accidents. In this sort of context the teacher's action and reaction are more driven by intuition rather than deliberate reflective thinking about alternative courses of action.

Another factor that makes advice about classroom tactics unreliable is the fact that different teachers can use apparently contradictory tactics with equal success!

So suggestions must be offered tentatively, recognising that many of the suggestions are based on experience, and may not match the experience of others. It is simply hoped that some of the suggestions may prove useful to some teachers!

Design and establish good starting routines for lessons

- ☐ Make sure that the room and resources are in a state of readiness.
- ☐ Arrive before the students, if you can.
- ☐ *Teach them* what is expected of them on arrival. For class teaching the permanent instruction might be: *Collect a copy of each item laid out on the resources table near the door. Have your rough book open and ready.* For independent or group work the instructions might be: *Collect the materials you are currently using and resume work.* At the beginning of the lesson the teacher's role should be purely supervisory and students should be

instructed to defer any individual approach to the teacher, except in emergency. A clear signal should be agreed which marks the end of this brief but vital period. During this supervision the teacher controls as much as possible by the eyes. Avoid speaking if possible; use the eyes and a few hand gestures.

Establish a clear understanding about 'speaking' rules

- ☐ There must be a clear signal that the teacher wishes to speak to the whole class. And that signal must mean three things: *stop talking; put down any materials or equipment; and listen.* Always use the same words as the signal. Make an issue of it whenever the signal is ignored. The younger secondary students enjoy practising these little routines, and they become conditioned to them. If you are trying to introduce the idea to older students it is more difficult. But quiet persistence pays off.

- ☐ During class teaching, whether in the form of class dialogue or in active learning, there needs to be clear understanding about the procedure for a student to speak. Simply to allow anyone to shout out contributions soon leads to chaos, and it is a poor training in responsible discussion. In class dialogue the old-fashioned *hands up* procedure works well enough. In active learning, organised in teams, the use of a *spokesperson* for a team is strongly recommended.

Develop clear routines for accomplishing regular organisational tasks

- ☐ These include taking the roll (if this is required), distributing materials in class teaching, clearing away at the end of lessons, forming groups, using apparatus. The way ahead in this is to make a mental note every time a small amount of chaos occurs. Consider what little routine might help to stop that occurring again.

Adopt a purely supervisory role at regular intervals throughout a lesson

- ☐ We have already examined this as an important component in the supervised study system. But the teacher is really supervising all the time! The danger in supervised study is to become too absorbed in helping a small group so that standards in the class

generally begin to slip. Short supervisory stints can help - a quick
scan of the whole room with a brief intervention wherever it
might seem necessary.

All control actions should be as unobtrusive as possible

☐ Some teachers can wither with a glance! It is worth being able to
do it! All gestures and signals can be effective: a finger to the
lips, a hand signal to sit down, a finger to beckon, a nod of
approval to allow something to happen, a shake of the head to say
no, a shake of the head to signal disapproval, an arm akimbo to
signal patience getting low. It can all be done **without saying a
word!**

☐ If it really is necessary to speak, approach the student and say it
quietly. The rest of the class is not disturbed, and if it is a
reprimand the student does not lose face and will accept it without
wanting to retaliate.

☐ If the general level of noise tends to escalate (and it usually does)
check it early on and unobtrusively. *Shsh!* can work wonders.
A quiet teacher makes a quiet class.

Continue to demonstrate your knowledge

☐ Always use a student's name.

☐ Make every encounter have at least one small personal touch in it.

Maintain the momentum and smoothness of the lesson

☐ Keep up the pace. Don't be long-winded. Don't *go on* about
inadequacies or misbehaviour. Don't over-elaborate an anecdote.
Don't over-teach the obvious.

☐ Don't interrupt the whole class during independent work with
instructions or exhortations. Don't keep *chopping and changing.*

Anticipate discipline problems and act quickly and decisively

☐ Alertness, anticipation, quick recognition, prompt but unobtrusive
action are the characteristics of the good disciplinarian. Where
the teacher is uncertain (and this is common) it is best to approach
to student in a non-critical way, asking the student to report what
progress has been made or what problems have been encountered.

This will get him or her back on task without the need for unsafe accusations.

☐ Where the misbehaviour is overt it is best to remove the student from any possible audience. Set the student to work in a different part of the room, making it clear that the student can return to base when the particular task is completed. This helps the student to accept the arrangement.

Avoid confrontation

☐ Confrontation is public and emotionally charged. It can result in frightful escalation with an unwillingness to back down on either side. It is usually watched with fascination by the rest of the class.

☐ An openly defiant student should be removed from the classroom and it is to be hoped that most schools have arrangements so that this can be arranged with supervision. The teacher will then have the opportunity to deal with the problem privately and (probably by then) more calmly.

D   The Disruptive Student

In our imperfect world many classes contain one or two students who are constantly disruptive. They may exhibit a combination of these symptoms: unable to concentrate or persevere; noisy; physically restless; inclined to interfere with other students; quarrelsome; react emotionally if reprimanded; easily bored; easily defeated by difficulties; often believe they are being victimised; often want to be friendly to the teacher but seem unable to prevent themselves being cheeky or silly.

For many such students a major problem is one of low self-esteem. Effective **differentiation** and regular small group **tutorials** will help some of these. But there may be a number of *hard core* students for whom little works; they can do a lot of harm in a classroom.

The teacher is often forced to spend a disproportionate amount of time with them, and confrontations occur which bring an abrupt halt to the work of the whole class. How can one allocate time and effort? On the one hand there is the programme of study and the needs of a whole class of students; on the other hand the disruptive student clearly needs some special attention.

Quite clearly, outside help may be required and may be available. But meanwhile the teacher needs to develop a strategy for the problem.

The lesson by lesson handling of the disruptive student needs to be guided by the general tactics already discussed, but in a systematic and deliberate way. The idea of teaching good behaviour, known as behaviour modification, has gained some acceptance. The argument is simply that the teacher does not have the time or resources to tackle the underlying causes, but can at least concentrate on trying to teach good behaviour. The system relies heavily on systematic reinforcement - mainly rewards for good behaviour. Because the causes of the disruptive behaviour are mainly beyond the reach of reason, the modification takes place through experience rather than through reasoned argument.

A programme for a disruptive student might be developed on these lines:

1) Find out what rewards might be valued by the student. This will vary according to age and interests - praise, privileges, reports, material rewards, tokens.

2) Make specific agreements about behaviour over short periods of time, with a clear understanding about the rewards.

3) Do a formal check and, if the standard has been reached, make the award.

4) Try to arrange that the tasks that the student prefers and finds pleasing should follow tasks which are not preferred. The pleasant tasks are then seen as a reward for the completion of the unpleasant.

5) Try to enlist the support of team members. If the reward is for the team then it is likely that the student will get a lot of help and encouragement.

6) Use negative reinforcement sparingly. Public reprimands will be counter-productive.

7) Give attention to the student when behaviour is good; withhold it when it is bad. This is a counsel of perfection, but it is important to have it always in mind, because the instinctive reaction is to do the exact opposite. Remember that the disruptive student wants attention. So spend more time reviewing good work and behaviour, in a more public way and with a show of friendship. Always deal with bad work and bad behaviour privately, briefly, and without too much fuss.

The Improvement of Classroom Management

THE IMPROVEMENT OF CLASSROOM MANAGEMENT

We have argued that teaching is a complex business, and that is the justification for the concept of classroom management.

So we have to accept that improvement of such a complex business requires deliberate and purposeful action. It will not happen by wishing, or by occasional *drives*. It needs to be planned as a long-term, regular, sustained programme of activities which become part of the teacher's way of life.

It is best if this can be arranged on a team basis because the benefits of shared thinking, group planning, mutual aid, and mutual criticism are substantial. Ideally the team should be a real team within the school organisation, for example, a secondary school faculty or department. But much can also be accomplished by a small *ad hoc* team set up informally. A partnership of two or three teachers who have similar responsibilities and who share a commitment to the improvement of their teaching, will accomplish a lot. Likewise a small *cluster group* of teachers from neighbouring schools can become a significant force for improvement. To work entirely alone must be regarded as the last resort, but it is better to do that than to drift into complacency or defeatism.

A ## Setting up an Evaluation Programme

Establishing the Group

In an ideal world the team would be an existing team within a school. The idea of setting up a programme for the improvement of teaching would spring naturally out of a debate which is a normal part of the team's processes. There might be some dissatisfactions with present practice. There might be a perceived opportunity springing from consideration of the implications of the National Curriculum.

The part played by the leader of the team in the early stages will be a critical factor. It may be necessary to extend awareness among the team members and to build up interest and commitment. In some teams the proposed programme might appear as a threat, and this needs to be handled with great care. Ultimately team members are going to have to adopt an approach which is rigorous and self-critical and which is capable of listening to criticism made by others. Time needs to be given to such anxieties; they cannot just be brushed aside. Much should be done by example rather than by exhortation. The support and advice of people outside the team should be sought, but with a sensitive appreciation of the extent to which this might increase the sense of threat among the team members.

Team members should be able to determine their own contribution to the programme. Some may be eager to get thoroughly involved in all the programme activities, but others, for one reason or another, may prefer a more limited role. The latter group may well lack confidence, but if their modest contribution is accepted and valued they will still be part of the team and will be able to extend their activities at a later date without having to do a *U turn*.

Time and effort given to team-building will pay off. The programme should not proceed until everyone in the team is committed to it, even if the commitment is very small scale.

Devising a Policy for Good Teaching and Learning

The team cannot make any progress until there is some kind of agreement about the aims and objectives of the programme. If we are setting out to improve the quality of teaching we need to get agreement about what constitutes *good* teaching. But is it not a fact that teaching styles differ and who is to say that one style is *better* than another?

The problem seems to be an intractable one. Yet we can be much more optimistic than appears possible at first. To begin with, a debate about what constitutes good teaching is a desirable thing in its own right. We ought not to evade it simply because it might reveal different perceptions. Second, when teachers get down to detail there is often more agreement than an early general discussion might have suggested. Third, the production of a policy for teaching can be a quicker exercise that many people initially expect. So the message must be to get started.

The ideal policy has these characteristics:

- it enjoys the commitment of all the members of a team of teachers
- it is based on systematic study of relevant guidelines
- it responds to local conditions, policies and developments
- it has been produced as a team effort.

The policy should always be regarded as *provisional*. This partly explains why a team can produce one quickly. It is provisional and will be brought up to date and improved regularly in the light of experience. In no sense is it a once and for all, state of the art, tablet of stone! There are bound to be new influences, new pressures, new ideas. And there are bound to be second thoughts based on experience of using the policy.

The policy should occupy pride of place in the team's documentation. It should be displayed prominently, shown to visitors, given to newcomers. It should have a place on the agendas of the team's regular meetings.

So what might such a policy look like? A model is outlined below.

B A Policy for Teaching and Learning: A Model Framework

An Outline Model

The first step is to determine the main headings under which we might describe the teaching objectives within the team. This will give us a framework for the detail of the policy. In discussion to determine these headings we shall need to bear two principles in mind:

☐ The headings must provide a comprehensive coverage so that all the objectives and associated activities can be included within the statement of the policy.

☐ The headings should not overlap each other. This is easy to say and almost impossible to achieve entirely. But it needs attention so that the worst overlaps are avoided.

When the headings have been determined then each should be defined by a short statement of the general aim. Based on the ideas developed in this book an example of a framework for a policy of teaching now follows. Note that the general aim which follows each heading is expressed as an assertion.

1   The Classroom

The classroom is attractive in appearance and functional.

2   Planning and Preparation

There is evidence of sound planning based on appropriate guidelines. This is backed by detailed and thorough preparation.

3   Learning Resources

The classroom has resources of sufficient quantity, quality, and variety in order to give maximum support to the teaching programme.

4   The Teacher as Leader and Presenter

The teacher demonstrates personal attributes, technical competencies, and subject knowledge that will promote the students' learning in an atmosphere of respect and confidence.

5   The Students as Active and Independent Learners

The students take an active part in the lessons and demonstrate their developing independence and sense of responsibility.

6   The Classroom Social System

The students have the opportunity to work as members of small groups, in pairs, and individually.

7   The Intellectual Climate

The teacher constantly raises the intellectual level of the verbal exchanges which take place in the classroom.

8   The Inter-personal Climate

The teacher and the students enjoy each other's company, are mutually supportive, and treat each other with courtesy and respect.

9   Management and Control

The teacher operates an efficient system of management and control. This rests on firm arrangements and on appropriate procedures.

10 The Management of Time

The teacher and the students get the most out of the time available through a well-developed sense of priorities and a sense of economy in the expenditure of time.

These headings need to be thoroughly discussed before proceeding further. Clearly individual teams will have their own different ideas as to how their work can best be classified, but it is hoped that the examples given above will serve as a model, and for many will also serve as a basis for a framework, requiring only a few modifications.

The Detailed Model

Armed with a set of headings and general aims we are now ready to fill in the detail. The recommended method is to take each heading in turn and ask the simple question: *What would an observer actually see in the classroom to suggest that the broad aim is being achieved?* In other words we are looking for **indicators.** We can express these best as assertions, in the same style as the general aims except that these will be much more detailed and specific. Our indicators should be, as far as possible, both observable and incontrovertible. But inevitably value judgements will have to be involved. Teaching does not lend itself to simple, mechanistic assessment.

The headings of our model are now repeated with suggested indicators appended.

1 The Classroom

The classroom is attractive in appearance and functional

1 The room is clean and tidy, occupied only by equipment and materials in current use.

2 Wall displays are attractively arranged and are relevant to the current teaching and learning.

3 Relevant reading and reference material is available to students at all times, without the need to request it.

4 The layout of furniture gives students as much work space as possible, and allows for flexibility between individual work, small group work and class teaching.

5 There is an adequate supply of all the writing and drawing materials and equipment that the students are likely to require.

6 The resources for learning currently in use are stored in such a way as to permit quick retrieval.

7 Adequate equipment is available to permit the projection of slides and filmstrips, and the playback of audio-tapes.

8 When required there is access to TV, radio, OHP, and computer facilities.

9 There are clear policies, rules, and procedures relating to the shared use of the room by several teachers.

10 There is a set of house rules governing the use of the room and its facilities by students when teaching is not taking place.

2 Planning and Preparation

There is evidence of sound planning based on appropriate guidelines. This is backed by detailed and thorough preparation.

1   There is a clear statement about the place of the programme of learning within the guidelines of the National Curriculum

2   More detailed educational objectives have been derived from the statement of broad aims laid down by the programme of study.

3   There is a detailed summary of the content of the programme.

4   There is a description of the kinds of learning activities which are intended for each stage in the programme.

5   Explicit arrangements have been made for the evaluation of the programme.

6   Appropriate learning resources have been carefully assembled and organised.

7   Some guidance material (eg. written or taped assignments, study guides) has been prepared in advance.

8   Documents have been prepared to assist the teacher in classroom management (eg. a teacher's guide, a desk plan).

9   Appropriate tests have been written or acquired.

10   There is a good stock of teacher presentation materials (eg. audio-visual aids, copies of handouts).

3 Learning Resources

The classroom has resources of sufficient quantity, quality, and variety in order to give maximum support to the teaching programme.

1   Resources are differentiated to match the needs of individual students (particularly with regard to reading levels of printed materials).

2   Quantities of resource items have been determined by the needs of the programme (eg: class sets; small sets; individual copies).

3   Printed resources have design appeal, in addition to providing the necessary data and stimuli.

4   Resources are classified and stored in a way that helps the students find and use them.

5   Resources are diverse, so that students can learn through visual and aural experiences as well as reading alone.

6   There are, as appropriate, specimens, models, artefacts, etc.

7   There are explicit arrangements for the students to use the central library/resources provision in the school.

8   Contacts with any local providers of resources have been made.

9   The teacher has access to sources of information which will support the work.

10 Students display a high level of competence in the handling and use of resources.

4 The Teacher as Leader and Presenter

The teacher demonstrates personal attributes, technical competencies, and subject knowledge that will promote the students' learning in an atmosphere of respect and confidence.

1 The teacher's mood is normally patient and good humoured.

2 The teacher creates a constant impression of self-confidence and self-control.

3 The teacher shows flexibility and an ability to respond creatively to events.

4 The teacher's instructions, descriptions and explanations are brief and clear.

5 As a result of the teacher's skills as discussion leader, the students demonstrate a high level of participation.

6 The teacher uses effective questioning in order to raise the level of students' thinking.

7 The teacher's voice is used in varied, interesting, and encouraging ways.

8 The language used by the teacher is carefully measured for its accuracy and for its appropriateness.

9 The teacher demonstrates a sound knowledge of the subject matter.

10 The teacher draws on a large repertoire of example, illustration, anecdote, and vivid detail.

5 The Students as Active and Independent Learners

The students take an active part in the lessons and demonstrate their developing independence and sense of responsibility.

1 When students arrive at the beginning of the lesson they take active steps to prepare for work.

2 Students display initiative in finding the resources and equipment they need.

3 Students display initiative in getting help with difficulties before seeking help from the teacher.

4 Students take an active part in discussion in a measured and responsible way.

5 Students frequently offer help to fellow students.

6 Students are often organised in teams as a way of supporting their active and independent learning.

7 Students frequently follow up classroom work with further investigation in the school library or elsewhere.

8 The teacher is able frequently to step back from the action because the students are all so involved and absorbed.

9 The teacher gives time to training the students in the skills of personal organisation and in the skills of learning.

10 Students accept substantial responsibility for the various *housekeeping* tasks of the classroom.

6 The Classroom Social System

The students have the opportunity to work as members of small groups, in pairs, and individually.

1 Students experience a balance of teaching and learning activities, organised as a whole class, in small groups, in pairs, and as individuals.

2 Within the groups there is a strong sense of mutual support.

3 The teacher gives time to training the students in the skills of small group work.

4 Group size is small enough to ensure participation of all members, yet large enough to produce diversity of response.

5 The composition of the groups has taken into account ties of friendship and the need to produce diversity of style.

6 There is a wide range of tasks for performance in groups: problem solving; games and simulations; discussions.

7 The teacher has given the groups adequate guidance on the procedures and standards for group work.

8 All group work is conducted in a disciplined manner.

9 There are well-organised opportunities for groups to report the outcomes of their work.

10 Students demonstrate their developing skills in group work by respecting the views of others and by engaging in debate without quarrelling.

7 The Intellectual Climate

The teacher constantly raises the intellectual level of the verbal exchanges which take place in the classroom.

1   The teacher allows time for students to express their ideas and to expand on them.

2   The teacher sets a good example of higher levels of thought.

3   The teacher encourages those who attempt to express themselves in abstract terms.

4   The teacher phrases questions in ways which will provoke divergent responses from the students.

5   The teacher uses and encourages the students to use language in a caring and measured way, appropriate to the needs of the situation.

6   The students demonstrate a willingness to analyse knowledge and ideas.

7   The students demonstrate a capacity for developing and testing hypotheses in a thoughtful way.

8   The students are ready to criticise information and ideas in a constructive manner.

9   The students are not afraid to express value judgements and to have them discussed.

10 The students constantly seek to structure their knowledge and understanding in meaningful ways.

8 The Inter-personal Climate

The teacher and the students enjoy each other's company, are mutually supportive, and treat each other with courtesy and respect.

1 The teacher shows a personal interest in individual students for their own sake, beyond the needs of the immediate learning task.

2 The teacher actively fosters a sense of group cohesion in work and in discipline.

3 The teacher is courteous towards individual students.

4 The teacher makes frequent use of praise and encouragement, but in a measured and sensitive way.

5 The teacher frequently accepts a student's expression of feeling about the work or the organisation.

6 The teacher frequently accepts or uses ideas expressed by a student.

7 The students display their willingness to work cooperatively.

8 The students feel free to signal their difficulties and to alert the teacher to organisational mistakes and problems.

9 The teacher and students occasionally share their sense of humour.

10 Students sometimes disagree with the teacher in a mature and non-threatening manner.

9 Management and Control

The teacher operates an efficient system of management and control. This rests on firm arrangements and on appropriate procedures.

1   The teacher has established procedures for the monitoring of each student's work.

2   The teacher has established clear personal objectives and commitments for each student.

3   There is an efficient system for the continuous recording of each student's tasks, progress and achievements.

4   Feedback is given to the student in order that the student can build up knowledge about his/her own performance.

5   The teacher gives clear directions on task procedures and encourages students to understand the structure of the lesson and of the course.

6   Students are encouraged to help in decision making about the organisation of the work.

7   The teacher handles minor lapses in student behaviour in a competent way, demonstrating alertness, sure judgement, and confidence.

8   The teacher copes with the complexities of classroom life in a calm and confident way.

9   The smooth flow of classroom activities is maintained by the teacher, particularly when there is a transition from one mode to another.

10 The teacher uses positive reinforcement (praise, incentives, peer manipulation) to help overcome problems caused by disruptive students.

10 The Management of Time

The teacher and the students get the most out of the time available through a well-developed sense of priorities and a sense of economy in the expenditure of time.

1 The teacher succeeds in allocating a high proportion of the available time to academic work.

2 The students spend a high proportion of their time engaged on their learning tasks.

3 The students experience a high degree of success during their engaged time.

4 The teacher maintains a good balance in the use of time on supervisory, organisational, and teaching tasks.

5 A high proportion of the teacher's time is spent in 'substantive interaction' with the students (ie. explaining, questioning, describing, illustrating).

6 The teacher has eliminated unnecessary routines and activities from his/her own performance.

7 The teacher has delegated to students responsibilities and tasks that are within their competence.

8 Simple and speedy procedures have been devised for tackling routine events and recurring problems.

9 There is evidence that the teacher plans ahead so that time in lessons is used most effectively.

10 The teacher regularly reviews the conduct of lessons in terms of the effective use of time by both teacher and students.

C   Setting your own Policy for Teaching

The example above of a policy for teaching can be used either as a model to start thinking, or even more usefully, as the basis for a department's own policy.

We have already claimed that the first provisional policy for teaching could be produced quite quickly, and there is a lot to be said for doing just that. The policy is only an *instrument*. Although it may start life as less than perfect, it is better than no instrument at all, especially when its use can lead to improvements in its design.

So the suggestion is made that a department should allocate **two hours** (during an in-service day, for example) with the firm intention of producing a provisional policy for teaching. Here are some suggestions as to how this might be done by a departmental team.

1)   The first task is to establish the framework of headings with their broad statement of aims. In order to do this, each member of the team should have access to the model provided in this chapter.

- Get each member to work privately for a short time in order to suggest a framework. Many of the headings given in the model may prove acceptable; others will need to be changed.

- After a brief period for private work go through the model's list of headings, and agree to adopt or reject and replace or modify each in turn.

- You should aim to have your own list of headings within half an hour. If debate gets too fierce remind members that they are only producing a **first draft**, not a statement for all time!

2)   Then allow members to work in pairs with each pair taking the responsibility for suggesting **indicators** for one or two headings (depending on your numbers). Suggest that they use the model to provide some of the ideas.

- Go through the model's list and accept, reject, or modify each indicator. They will almost certainly wish to develop some indicators which more accurately represent the needs and aspirations of the department.

- They could be advised to do this through an initial brainstorm to provide as big a bank of ideas as possible, leaving the critical analysis of them until later.

- Ask them to be ready to report **within an hour.**

3) Use the last half hour to receive and accept or modify the reports from the pairs.

- Encourage people to be generous and not too fussy (first draft!).
- Aim to have a document ready for typing by the end of the half hour.

Of course it is too rushed. But isn't all teaching like that? The point is that there is now a tool, however imperfect, waiting to be used. And that is what we must think about now.

D   **Evaluating Existing Practice**

We are now ready to put into practice the cycle of improvement described in the introduction to this book. Here are the steps.

Step 1 : Prepare an evaluation of the teaching as it exists now.

Use the department's policy for teaching as the agenda for a meeting. Try to arrive at some conclusions under each of the headings.

Step 2 : Identify key areas for improvement.

This could be done at the same meeting as Step 1, but there could be an advantage in giving time for reflection and devoting more time to Step 2. The size of the key areas is a matter for personal decision. On one occasion a department might decide to cover a **number of areas** for improvement, accepting that each part could only be given **limited attention**. On another occasion the department might decide to concentrate a **lot of time and effort** on **one specific aspect** of the policy.

Step 3 : Formulate plans for improvement.

The team should decide upon specific objectives for improvement and consider appropriate strategies.

This step need not take long, because the indicators already listed in the policy could provide ready-made objectives. But it may be desirable to work out more detail, and to give some idea of the actual location of the improvements within the departments and work, and also some idea of the time scale involved.

Step 4 : Decide how the evaluation will be conducted.

Teachers could certainly report on their conclusions about their own work. But, if it can be arranged, the **observation** of each other's work can be very valuable. We are going to discuss this separately in the next section. Other useful sources of evidence can be from independent observers and from the students themselves.

E ## Mutual Observation

This must surely be the most fruitful approach to the improvement of teaching and learning. There is increasing acceptance that the isolation of the teacher in the classroom is harmful, both from a personal point of view and from the point of view of the profession as a whole.

Comparisons can be made with other professions where to observe and to be observed are regarded as an essential part of the initial training and subsequent development of the individual member. Opening up the classroom has become a commonly expressed desire. The initial idea is often little more than a feeling that if teachers could only *drift* in and out of each other's classrooms a lot of knowledge about each other's styles and techniques would be picked up, casually and almost accidentally. The idea seems attractive and not potentially threatening.

We need however to be much more disciplined and purposeful than this. The use of a policy for teaching is one way of getting started. There are some points to be made.

- [ ] This is observation for mutual support and improvement, **not** teacher appraisal.
- [ ] All observation should be conducted on a mutual basis and on terms of equality. If a head of department wishes to observe members of the department, the best way to start is to invite the members to observe the head of department first.
- [ ] The nature of an observation should always be determined by objectives that have been chosen by the teacher to be observed.
- [ ] Results from an observation are the property of the observed.
- [ ] Observation must always be followed by a discussion between the observer and the observed.

It is worth mentioning briefly that in addition to using a policy for teaching as the basis for mutual observation, a department could decide to use one of the published systems. Many such systems have been devised, mainly by research workers. For example, one of the oldest and best known is the *Flanders Interaction Analysis*. This is valuable where a teacher is engaged in whole class teaching and wishes to test the amount and kinds of student involvement. The system can be used in a very simple way, or it can be more elaborate leading to a very sophisticated analysis of classroom interactions. Interested teachers should consult **Flanders N (1970)**. *Analysing Teaching Behaviour.* Addison-Wesley.

Of course there are difficulties in getting all this into place. The tightness of school timetables does not help. But mutual observation is so important that it should be given priority, perhaps using supply cover for the purpose in preference to using it to send teachers outside to courses. Another valuable possibility comes from the increasing number of **advisory teachers** now being appointed by local authorities whose brief is to support the developments in teaching and learning by working with teachers in the schools. The quality of much work done under this arrangement has been extraordinarily high.

F Some Final Points

Adopting a systematic approach to the improvement of teaching is not necessarily a sure guarantee of instant success. There may be some failures on the way and some disappointments. A few suggestion may help.

Look wide for support

Working entirely alone can be dispiriting. Making improvements needs helpers - personal counsellors; experts; those who control the money.

Give the programme a sustained effort

Don't give up at the first signs of difficulty. Classroom improvements often come about slowly, but they will yield to persistence.

Avoid 'programmitis'

This is getting more interested in the programme than the things that it is supposed to serve. The symptoms are: too many meetings; too much documentation; rigid procedures; the exclusion of any activity which does not fit into the programme.

Aim high

It is worth it to go all out to make a real difference. This often means concentrating one's efforts. But when substantial differences are made morale is given a great boost; and other people take notice. So **aim high**!

APPENDIX A Selected List of References

Brighouse T (1990). What Makes a Good School? Network Educational Press.

Department of Education and Science (1988). Secondary Schools: An Appraisal by HMI. HMSO

Department of Education and Science (1979). Mixed Ability Work in Comprehensive Schools. HMSO.

Duke D (ed.) (1979). Classroom Management. The 78th Yearbook of the National Society for the Study of Education. NSSE.

Dunkin M and Biddle B (1974). The Study of Teaching. Holt, Reinehart and Winston.

Gage N (ed.) (1976). The Psychology of Teaching Methods. The 75th Yearbook of the National Society for the Study of Education. NSSE.

Hopson B and Scally M (1980). Lifeskills Teaching. McGraw Hill.

Lewis R (1986). The Schools Guide to Open Learning. NEC.

Lincoln P (1987). The Learning School. British Library.

Marland M (1981). Information Skills in the Secondary School Curriculum. Methuen Educational.

Miller J (1982). Tutoring: the Guidance and Counselling Role of the Tutor in Vocational Preparation. FEU.

NEC/NCET (1989). Implementing Flexible Learning: A Resource Pack for Trainers.

Powell R (1990). Resources for Flexible Learning. Network Educational Press.

Reid M, Clunies-Ross L, Goacher B, and Vile C (1981). Mixed Ability Teaching. NFER-Nelson.

TVEI (1989). Developments 10: Flexible Learning. Training Agency.

US Department of Education (1986). What Works: Research about Teaching and Learning. US Department of Education.

Waterhouse P (1988). Supported Self-Study: An Introduction for Teachers. NCET.

Waterhouse P (1990). Flexible Learning: An Outline. Network Educational Press.

Waterhouse P (1990). Tutoring. Network Educational Press.

Index

The Teaching and Learning Series

This book, *Classroom Management,* is the second in the series and is closely related to four others which examine important issues both for the classroom teacher and the school or college manager.

Book 1, *Flexible Learning: An Outline,* by **Philip Waterhouse,** provides an outline of all the key questions in the debate on teaching and learning styles. He examines the rationale, contexts and methods of *flexible learning:*

- The National Curriculum
- Assessment
- TVEI
- Records of Achievement
- Study skills
- Tutoring
- The flexible use of space, time, money and people
- The use of libraries and resource centres

Flexible Learning: An Outline is a **handbook**. Each chapter provides an agenda, a checklist of key issues and will be invaluable to all those interested in stimulating discussion or raising awareness on the subject of how teachers teach and how students learn.

ISBN 1 85539 003 5 £4.50 Published May 1990

Book 3, *Resources for Flexible Learning,* by **Robert Powell,** provides practical advice on the complex question of Resources.

- Defining *flexible* resources
- Choosing and evaluating resources
- Adapting existing resources
- Making full use of libraries/resource centres
- Preparing study guides
- Planning and writing assignments
- Thinking about design and layout
- Using desktop publishing.

The book will suggest ways in which teachers and students can use a wide variety of resources both to satisfy the demands of the National Curriculum and to develop independent learning skills.

ISBN 1 85539 005 1 £4.50 To be published October 1990

Book 4, *Tutoring,* by **Philip Waterhouse** explores the possibilities of skilful tutoring. It presents clearly:

- The *rationale* and *objectives* of tutoring
- The *contexts* for tutoring
- *Arrangements* for tutoring
- Tutoring *styles*
- Tutoring *techniques*.

The book will serve as an invaluable handbook for all those seeking to provide guidance and support to students both in the classroom and in more informal learning situations.

ISBN 1 85539 006 X   £4.50   To be published November 1990

Book 5, *What makes a Good School?* by **Tim Brighouse** identifies those features of school organisation and management which are essential elements of successful teaching and learning. It examines:

- Leadership in the successful school
- Environment in the successful school
- Staff development in the successful school
- Collective review in the successful school
- School and curriculum development planning
- The organisation of learning in the successful school
- Successful teaching and learning.

ISBN 1 85539 007 8   £4.50   To be published November 1990

This book is an introduction to a major series by **Tim Brighouse** *(Research Machines Professor of Education, University of Keele)* which explores each of the topics above in some depth. This series will be published by Network Educational Press in 1991.

All books in the *Teaching and Learning* series £4.50; discounts available for bulk orders direct from the publishers. Order forms and further details from:
Network Educational Press, PO Box 635, Stafford, ST18 OLJ
Telephone: 0889 271300

Other Titles from Network Educational Press

Coursework Enquiry/Study Guides
introduced by **Philip Waterhouse**

A series of photocopiable coursework enquiry/study guides is available in the following subject areas:

- Geography
- Humanities
- Business Studies

Each subject pack contains 30 different enquiries on a wide range of topics. The guides provide:

- clear, practical guidance
- advice on resources, activities and presentation
- scope for individual group or class investigations
- flexibility in use.

50,000 of these guides have been purchased by schools and colleges since their publication in May 1989. They have been purchased for use in:

- Geography, Humanities and Business Studies *(13-16)*
- English *(13-16)*
- General Studies *(14-18)*
- Personal and Social Education *(14-18)*
- CPVE *(16+)* and B TEC. *(16+)*

Each pack £35.00. A full set of Geography, Humanities and Business Studies £95.00. Brochures and order forms from the publishers,

Forthcoming titles

The success of the study guides has led us to increase the range of subjects. During the Spring Term 1991 guides will be published in:

- Technology (200 from a range of disciplines)
- History
- English Language
- Science

Details of all these publications from:
Network Educational Press, PO Box 635, Stafford, ST18 OLJ
Tel: 0889 271300

English Literature

Activities / Assignments Guides

A series of photocopiable guides which support flexible styles of teaching and learning in English Literature.

□ **16 titles in the range**

The guides provide a fresh and imaginative approach to English literature and will appeal to:

- experienced teachers looking for new ideas
- teachers new to particular texts
- student teachers
- non - specialists.

Each guide has 3 sections:

- a summary of key plot events (for easy reference)
- a collection of varied learning activities
- a collection of assignments.

The activities seek to develop a wide range of student skills:

- oral skills
- paired and small group work
- improvisation and role play
- discursive, narrative and creative writing.

The assignments engage the student in a detailed study of the text, are clearly differentiated, and seek to provide:

- a critical understanding of plot, character and style
- suggestions for the open study or extension work
- scope for independent research
- coursework opportunities in English.

Published **November 1990**   £24.00 per photocopiable pack.

Available from the publishers:
Network Educational Press, PO Box 635, Stafford, ST18 OLJ